GOD IS GREATER THAN FAMILY MESS

REVISED & UPDATED

GOD IS GREATER THAN FAMILY MESS

How God Uses Family Mess As a Vehicle of Our Destiny

Bishop Joey Johnson

REVISED & UPDATED

GOD IS GREATER THAN FAMILY MESS

Cover Design by Atinad Designs

© Copyright 2009

SAINT PAUL PRESS, DALLAS, TEXAS
First Printing, 2003
Second Printing, 2009

ISBN-13: 978-0-9825303-4-4

Printed in the U.S.A.

PRAISE for
GOD IS GREATER THAN FAMILY MESS

"My friend, Joey Johnson, has done all of us a great favor! Read this book for a fresh grip on a great home and a compelling glimpse of a great God."

–Joseph Stowell, President
Moody Bible Institute

"Joey Johnson is a leader whose pastoral vision is wise and compassionate, whose leadership is prophetic and biblically centered, whose passion is for a Spirit-filled, Christ-exalting Church, and whose integrity is pure and proven. I commend his ministry as well as his new book, *God Is Greater Than Family Mess*."

–Jack W. Hayford, Litt. D.
Pastor/Chancellor
The Church On The Way
The King's Seminary
Van Nuys, California

"There are some books that are written just to be written and others that ought to be written but never are, but this book had to be written, and thank God it has been. With the skill of a scholar, the passion of a preacher and the profundity and perspective of a pastor, Joey Johnson has exposed and revealed the Family Mess that so many live with, struggle with and seek to hide and avoid. This book speaks to where we are and how we live, but will not let us be content to stay there. Pastor Joey assures us that God can turn the mess into a miracle. Read this book and be blessed, read it and be helped, read it and be changed."

–Bishop Timothy J. Clark
First Church of God, City of Refuge
Columbus, Ohio

"Journey with Joey Johnson through the family histories of the Bible to discover your own family history today."

–Leith Anderson, President
National Association of Evangelicals
Washington, D.C.

"With the abundance of books published on the topic of family, it would seem to be next to impossible to say anything fresh or innovative. Pastor Johnson has accomplished the 'next to impossible.' Not only is his insight into family life and family dysfunction fresh, it is also thoroughly biblical. You'll never read the book of Genesis the same way again. This is a very welcome and much needed addition to Christian literature on the family."

–Rich Nathan
Senior Pastor
Vineyard Columbus

CONTENTS

ACKNOWLEDGEMENTS

I want to thank and give honor to my God, Who has used me in spite of my sins because He has an eternal destiny for me.

I want to thank my wife, Cathy, for her long years of support and encouragement in an exciting, growing, and demanding ministry.

Thanks to my dedicated staff for their labor of love alongside me, and the people of my church for their prayers, support, and suggestions.

My sincere thanks to the men of God who have supported me and this book.

DISCLAIMER

In treating the story of Abraham and his generations using the concept of family mess, I am purposefully and as sensitively as possible, looking at the people, their stories, and their cultural situations through American lenses. When this is done unknowingly and pejoratively, it involves ethnocentrism and anachronism. Ethnocentrism is reading back into the texts and contexts of the Bible our own culture, while anachronism is reading our own times back into the texts and contexts of the Bible. Ethnocentrism (historical eisegesis)[1] is imagining that all people everywhere and at all times think as I do.[2]

Because I have a graduate level reading certification in cultural anthropology and New Testament interpretation, I'm aware of the fact the people who populate the pages of the Bible are not Americans and they do not think as I do. In fact, they are collectivistic as opposed to individualistic. They are non-psychological, as opposed to psychological. And they are non-introspective, as opposed to introspective—to name a few of the major differences in biblical culture and American culture.

Therefore, I realize that the people who populate the pages of the Bible were not concerned with the pop psychology of dysfunctionality.

However, having done a great deal of reading and studying of the culture of the Bible, the first-century circum-Mediterranean culture in particular, I have sought to understand the original perspectives and truths of the stories and then update those perspectives and truths by looking at them through American lenses. Many scholars do this with little awareness of the cultural differences. I do this with a full awareness of the differences.

Consequently, reading the text with as much sensitivity as possible, I offer these considerations.

AUTHOR'S PREFACE

This book grew out of a series called "Family Mess," which I preached in 1997 at my church, The House of the Lord, in Akron, Ohio. As I preached a single message or multiple messages from this series at other churches, I've been greatly humbled and amazed by the number of people who have experienced the healing touch of God through these teachings. The demand for tapes and requests for sermon notes revealed the need to put this series into book form.

There are twelve chapters, each with discussion questions that are ideal for quarterly Sunday school studies or home Bible groups.

I pray that God will use this book to help you acknowledge the fact that family mess happens. I pray that by acknowledging this, the Holy Spirit will bring to your remembrance painful events that need to be felt, processed, grieved, forgiven, and released. I pray that this process will bring you face-to-face with the living God, with the realization that He is greater than family mess, and that He works in spite of, through, beneath, above, and beyond family mess to give you an eternal destiny!

–Bishop Joey Johnson
Akron, Ohio

CHAPTER 1

The Long-Term Impact of Family Mess
(As the World Turns)

The longer I live, the more I learn. The more I learn, the more I know there is to learn. The more I see that there is to learn, the more I realize how little time I have to learn what God wants me to learn and apply.

One of the truths that concerns me greatly is the long-term impact of families upon their members. This impact can be good or bad, but the negative impact is particularly devastating. This is poignantly pointed out in the Bible. As a matter of fact, one of the Scriptures that I am thinking about is repeated four times in God's Word.

> "You shall not make for yourself an idol, or any likeness of what is in heaven above or on the earth beneath or in the water under the earth. You shall not worship them or serve them; for I, the LORD your God, am a jealous God, *visiting the iniquity of the fathers on the children, on the third and the*

fourth generations of those who hate Me" (Exodus 20:4-5, emphasis mine).

Then the LORD passed by in front of him and proclaimed, "The LORD, the LORD God, compassionate and gracious, slow to anger, and abounding in lovingkindness and truth; who keeps lovingkindness for thousands, who forgives iniquity, transgression and sin; yet He will by no means leave the guilty unpunished, *visiting the iniquity of fathers on the children and on the grandchildren to the third and fourth generations*" (Exodus 34:6–7, emphasis mine).

"The LORD is slow to anger and abundant in lovingkindness, forgiving iniquity and transgression; but He will by no means clear the guilty, *visiting the iniquity of the fathers on the children to the third and the fourth generations*" (Numbers 14:18, emphasis mine).

"You shall not make for yourself an idol, or any likeness of what is in heaven above or on the earth beneath or in the water under the earth. You shall not worship them or serve them; for I, the LORD your God, am a jealous God, *visiting the iniquity of the fathers on the children, and on the third and the fourth generations of those who hate Me*" (Deuteronomy 5:8–9, emphasis mine).

As you can see, the operative phrase is *"visiting the iniquity of the fathers on the children to the third and fourth generations."* This is the phrase I want to concentrate on in this book.

First, we need to determine what God is not saying. He is not saying that He punishes the children for the sin of their parents. He clearly says so in Deuteronomy 24:16: *"Fathers shall not be put to death for their sons, nor shall sons be put to death for their fathers; everyone shall be put to death for his own sin."*

So, what *is* God saying?

Well, let's look at the meaning of the words and see if we can begin to understand what God is saying. First, the Hebrew word for *visiting* is *paqad,* which means to visit, either with friendly or hostile intent. Second, the Hebrew word for *iniquity* is *avon,* which means perversity, moral evil, fault, iniquity, mischief, punishment of iniquity, or sin.

So, God is saying that He is going to visit, or bring about, punishment for the sinfulness of a father to the third and fourth generation of that man's family. The word *punishment* in this context does not mean the inflicting of a penalty upon one for a crime or sin, but the suffering, pain, or loss that serves as retribution.[1] God is not discussing the punishment of a penalty, but the consequences of sin. Let's see if we can understand this more deeply.

God must, because of His nature, deal retribution to every human being. The word *retribution* means "just punishment for evil done or just reward for good done." So retribution can be either positive or negative depending upon the context. At the end of time, when God wraps everything up, He will give to every person his or her retribution. God must do this because of His immutable, unchanging, stable nature.

God is a holy God. He is a just God. He is a righteous God. Therefore, every sin must receive a just payment of reward, recompense, or retribution. Like the word *retribution,* the meaning of the words *recompense* and *reward,* when they are used in the Bible, must be determined by their usage.

Since we are all sinners, and our *self*-righteousness is nothing more than filthy rags, to pay for our sins we must be sentenced to hell. This is tragic indeed, but praise God that the Cross takes care of all the sins—past, present, and future with respect to salvation—of those who place their trust in Jesus Christ. Jesus' death upon the Cross takes care of the penalty of sin for those who place their faith in Him.

However, in the four passages of Scripture quoted above, God is not discussing personal sin, but *familial* sin. God is discussing the impact of sin upon succeeding generations. God is discussing the consequences of sin, both forgiven and unforgiven, upon the children who will come later.

The wonderful gift of God's forgiveness takes care of all sin—past, present, and future, with respect to salvation; but it does not wipe out the *consequences* of sin in this life. One day God will right every wrong and wipe away every tear from our eyes, but for now the consequences of sin are still with us. Therefore,

God must, because of His nature, visit the consequences of the father's sin upon the children to the third and fourth generation.

There is another reason why God must visit the consequences of the sins of fathers upon their children: God's nature is expressed in the laws of the earth that He has created.

For instance, Newton's Third Law of Motion is that for every action, there is an equal and opposite reaction. In the same way, there are consequences for righteousness and sin, and these consequences must be visited upon future generations. The Scriptures we are considering deal with the consequences for sin. It is not so much God personally visiting the consequences of sin upon succeeding generations, as it is the nature of the way that God has created things to operate—which is in keeping with His own nature.

Salvation takes care of the punishment for sin, but it does not take care of the specific impact of sin. Consequences are the normal, logical, natural, systematic results of an action. We are basically discussing cause and effect. For every cause there is some effect:

- If a fertile man and woman have sex, the effect is often a baby.
- If someone chooses to drink heavily for a long period of time, the effect is often cirrhosis of the liver.
- If a father commits sin, the effect is that some consequences of that sin will show up in his children in some way.

This is a law of heredity. Because of the disobedience of Adam, the stream of humanity is polluted and we all inherit the sin nature. All men are born in the sin that has been passed on to them from their parents, grandparents, etc. But how? Well, I'm no scientist, but I do know that man has come far enough in scientific study to know that genes control inheritance by transmitting one or more traits to one's offspring. The genes of the father are passed on to his offspring. In those genes is the genetic code of the father, which may actually include specific sinful impact.

You know that. You've sampled it scientifically. You have seen children who have not grown up with their father or even known their father, but they act just like their father. How could that be? How could that boy act so much like his father having never known his father? It's because it has been genetically passed on to him.

This brings us to the age-old question: What causes people to sin—their heredity (that which is inborn) or their environment (that which they experience)? Well, we shall see in the chapters to come that the answer is *both*. Children are impacted by the consequences of the father's sin—through both heredity and environmental influences. The percentage of impact depends upon many variables, but one thing is sure: The consequences of a father's sin are going to impact his offspring. Therefore, we see what God means when the Bible says He visits the iniquity (i.e. the consequences of sin) of the fathers upon the children to the third and fourth generations.

Perhaps the most striking aspect of this truth is the fact that sin has such far-reaching, long-term effects. Keep in mind these three familial impacts of sin:

1. *Sin always effects present devastation and bondage.* The sins of the father and the mother bring fairly immediate devastation and bondage both to the perpetrators and to the victims.

2. *Sin always reaches back to the past.* Present sin is somehow connected to sin that has been committed in the past. It is connected in heredity or environmental influence to someone or something in the past. Sin is never a single act disconnected from the larger continuum of human sin. Whatever sinful act we commit is connected to past generations, all the way back to Adam. This whole sequence of events got started in the Garden of Eden.

3. *Sin never stops with one generation.* Sin always reaches forward and touches our future posterity, our children. Somehow it always impacts the generations to come.

There is an excellent Minirth/Meier book entitled *Kids Who Carry Our Pain*.[2] The gist of it is that our children deal with and finish the pain in our lives that we didn't work through. But I would take it one step further: Kids not only carry our pain, *they also carry the consequences of our sin.* A lot of that pain exists as a result of the consequences of our sin.

That is easy to understand with devastating sins like abuse, alcoholism, or drug abuse. It is still true but much harder to see and understand with sins such as gluttony, selfishness, and pride.

Let me state this in terms that are easier for us to understand: Family sin leads to family mess!

When we say something is a mess, we mean that the situation is disorderly, confusing, muddled, troubling, difficult, untidy, dirty, and thus embarrassing. Disorder means a lack of normal order. This suggests the upset of the normal functions or health of something. Consequently, the word is strongly related to the concept of dysfunctionality. Therefore, family sin leads to family dysfunctionality—a family that is not functioning as it ought to function. It's a family mess!

Families in a mess have three patterns that members tend to follow:

1. *Don't talk.* Don't ever talk to anyone about the sin, abuse, or neglect that is going on in your family. Keep the family secrets. Generally, the sicker the family the more secrets there are that must be kept. I am not discussing the normal privacy of a healthy family, but the sick privacy of abuse.

2. *Don't feel.* Do whatever you have to do to keep from facing the pain of your situation. Use whatever substance, pattern, person, thing, or idea you need to stay out of the pain. Don't face the real pain because it will undo you. Everybody wants to just go on. But you can't go on

over family mess! It needs to be dealt with. When Nehemiah came to Jerusalem, not only were the walls broken down and the gates burned with fire, but there was also debris in the street. You can't build a city on debris—you need to clean up first. You can't just go on. Family mess needs to be dealt with.

3. *Don't trust.* You have been so devastated in your life that you cannot afford to trust anyone no matter how trustworthy a person might seem or how he might prove himself. This includes God! If people are untrustworthy, God must be, too.

As I stated earlier, our operative phrase occurs four times in God's Word. Some have said that four is the number of the earth. Family mess happens, even "As the World Turns!" It is not something you can avoid, but it is something that you can heal from.

The Bible is a real book that gives the real story of real people and their real interaction with the real God! Therefore, the Bible is full of family mess. God does not hide the truth; He deals with reality. There can be no healing or freedom from family mess until we face the reality of what has happened.

Take slavery, for instance. It is interesting to me that very few people seem to understand the ongoing impact of slavery upon the African-American community. If we go back three or four generations in our history, we come face-to-face with the ravages of slavery, and the American brand of slavery was one of the most dehumanizing forms of slavery known to humanity.

The family mess that was caused by slavery is still impacting us today. The three patterns of dysfunctional families apply to us: We still don't talk very freely; we still have difficulty feeling our real feelings; and we still have difficulty trusting one another, not to mention other ethnic groups.

But praise God, because He wants to deliver us from family mess. And He has experience in delivering people from the family mess of slavery. He delivered His chosen people, the Israelites, who had been in bondage in Egypt for 400 years.

God took the children of Israel out of Egypt in one night, but it took God forty years to get the immediate impact of slavery out of the children of Israel. And even after all the adults of that generation had died, the people were still suffering the long-term impact of their previous enslavement. I am not bringing this up to make excuses for African-American people. I am bringing this up so that we may understand the reality of the damage that has occurred and realistically seek God for deliverance and healing.

In His deliverance, God used both the *crisis* and the *process* of deliverance.

- *Deliverance from Egypt was a crisis.* It happened miraculously, in one night, at once, and once and for all. God closed the Red Sea behind them so they couldn't go back.

- *Deliverance from the effects of slavery was a process.* It took at least forty years in the wilderness, but probably additional time in the Promised Land.

God delivered African-Americans from slavery with the Emancipation Proclamation, though the Emancipation Proclamation has never been fully realized. Therefore, we are still struggling with the effects of slavery.

God took us out of the slavery of sin in the *crisis* of salvation. Jesus said that *"if the Son makes you free, you will be free indeed"* (John 8:36), but we are still struggling with the effects of sin. God is still taking slavery out of us in the *process* of progressive sanctification.

"As the World Turns" there is sin, family mess, and generational bondage. But there is also a God Who wants to bring hope, deliverance, and restoration! Can you believe that family mess can also be a divine messenger with a divine message?

- *God wants to use the suffering of our ethnicity to give a divine message of hope, deliverance, and restoration to the world.* When the world looks at African-American people and sees the hope, deliverance, and restoration that God has worked in us after the suffering of slavery, it will be a testimony to the power of Almighty God.

- *God wants to use the suffering of our ethnicity to give a divine message of compassion, deep feeling, devotion, and piety to this world.* God wants the world to look on black people and see our suffering and understand what compassion is all about.

- *God wants to use the suffering of our ethnicity to create "transethnic" communities to model love and reconciliation.* He wants to show the world what a true microcosm of Heaven would look like—red and yellow, black and white, worshiping God here on earth, right now, through the power of the Holy Spirit.

Let me summarize this chapter with five important truths:

1. *Family mess is the tip-off that there is something seriously wrong with your family.* Don't ignore it or say, "Well, you know, that's just the way we are." Pay attention to it.

2. *Family mess is the tip-off that there is something beyond natural circumstances impacting your family: generational bondage.* When you remember that your great-granddaddy was an alcoholic and you remember your grandfather was an alcoholic and you remember your father was an alcoholic, you need to pay attention to that pattern.

3. *Family mess is the tip-off that you need someone or something greater than you if you are going to be healed.*

Counseling is great, but only Jesus Christ can truly straighten out family mess.

4. *Family mess can alert you to areas of struggle or sin that you should be aware of.* This is like number two. If you're a woman and your great-grandmother always had three or four men hanging around, and your grandmother did too, and your mother did too, guess what sin you're going to have to watch out for in your own life?

5. *Family mess can alert you to areas of struggle or sin where God wants to work.* He wants to move right in at the deepest, most difficult part of your life to bring healing and transformation.

In the next chapter, we are going to follow the family mess in the family of God's chosen people, beginning with the patriarch, Abraham. We are going to see the impact of family mess as well as how God works to establish His chosen people in spite of it.

DISCUSSION QUESTIONS

1. Why must God visit the consequences of the fathers' sins upon their children? Please answer this question in your own words.

2. Are you aware of any family mess in your family? Can you share an experience that has negatively impacted your formation as a person?

3. How are you keeping or breaking the three patterns of family dysfunctionality?

4. Can you get in touch with anything that God might be trying to work out through the suffering of your particular family mess?

5. Can you think of any biblical or daily situation where God has given someone a destiny in spite of family mess?

CHAPTER 2

The Process Of Separation From Family Mess
(The Guiding Light)

In the first chapter of this book, we saw that family sin leads to family mess. God must visit the sins of the fathers upon the children. Now while this is obviously true, this does not necessarily cause family mess. So, what does cause family mess?

Well, let's touch on two causes:

1. Human depravity
2. Satan and his evil horde

Let's talk first about human depravity. Having the consequences of hereditary and environmental sin passed on to anyone is very serious, but it is human depravity that makes it family mess. Heredity and environmental forces are not the sole or even the primary determining factors in how a person is going to turn out.

We have bought into this idea that we're all messed up because of either our genes or our homes. But I'm here to tell you that there's something else behind our family mess.

The determining factor is still human will and choice. God holds us accountable for our choices even though we face some powerful influences. Don't worry; He knows that we are but dust! But it is human depravity, impacting our human will and choices that makes family mess.

Because of the fall—the sin of Adam who is the father of mankind—the whole human race is depraved (utterly sinful). Paul, speaking for God, put it like this:

> As it is written, "There is none righteous, not even one; there is none who understands, there is none who seeks for God; all have turned aside, together they have become useless; there is none who does good, there is not even one" (Romans 3:10–12).

We all receive the consequences of our forefather's sins. That's true. But it is our own depravity or utter wickedness that causes our individual *expression* of family mess. Our choices will be in keeping with the unique nature of our own personal depravity. Without Jesus Christ and the ongoing sanctifying ministry of the Holy Spirit, our choices cannot help but produce family mess.

This does not mean that there is nothing noble in human beings, because the image of God is still inside of us. But we are fallen image-bearers!

There is also another very powerful reason for family mess: sin. We have an enemy and his name is Satan. He is God's enemy and therefore he is our enemy. He is bent on taking the sin and the opportunities we give him and turning them into family mess in our lives. God allows this for His own sovereign purposes and His own ultimate, divine glory, until He brings everything to consummation at the end of the age.

So, I hope you are beginning to understand the phrase, *"visiting the iniquity of the fathers upon the children to the third and fourth generation."* I hope that you are beginning to understand the force behind it and the forces that are sometimes involved in it.

Now we want to begin to see how this phrase works its way out in the family of Abraham. The Bible gives us the important details of the life of Abraham. Malcolm Smith said this in his book, *Spiritual Burnout:*

> The Scripture is not a book of systematic theology that tabulates what we are to believe. It is a book of biographies that shows how very ordinary people, through the ages, have learned to walk in God's strength to overcome their problems. He shows how they discovered the reality of God in the black holes of their personal failures.[1]

Abraham was the friend of God. He was chosen by God to be a great example of faith, the father of many nations, the father of the Israelites, and the father of the genealogical life of the Messiah, Jesus Christ.

Now these are the records of the generations of Terah. Terah became the father of Abram, Nahor and Haran; and Haran became the father of Lot. Haran died in the presence of his father Terah in the land of his birth, in Ur of the Chaldeans. Abram and Nahor took wives for themselves. The name of Abram's wife was Sarai; and the name of Nahor's wife was Milcah, the daughter of Haran, the father of Milcah and Iscah. Sarai was barren; she had no child. Terah took Abram his son, and Lot the son of Haran, his grandson, and Sarai his daughter-in-law, his son Abram's wife; and they went out together from Ur of the Chaldeans in order to enter the land of Canaan; and they went as far as Haran, and settled there. The days of Terah were two hundred and five years; and Terah died in Haran.

Now the LORD said to Abram, "Go forth from your country, And from your relatives And from your father's house, To the land which I will show you; And I will make you a great nation, And I will bless you, And make your name great; And so you shall be a blessing; And I will bless those who bless you, And the one who curses you I will curse. And in you all the families of the earth will be blessed."

So Abram went forth as the LORD had spoken to him; and Lot went with him. Now Abram was seventy-five years old when he departed from Haran. Abram took Sarai his wife and Lot his nephew, and all their possessions which they had accumulated, and the persons which they had acquired in Haran, and they set out for the land of Canaan; thus they came to the land of Canaan (Genesis 11:27–12:5).

Here we get the background of Abraham. (His name was actually Abram at this point since this was before God changed his name to Abraham. But for convenience and familiarity, let's call him Abraham.) Here we see the Lord God's call upon his life. And here is where the family sin begins.

Ur of the Chaldeans was in ancient Babylonia, and the worship of idols and false gods was very big in Babylonia. We know from Joshua 24:2 that Terah, Abraham's father, served other gods. Remember, family sin leads to family mess. But God stepped into the midst of this family sin, this idolatry, and called Abraham. God gave Abraham something that no one in his family had apparently experienced before: "A Guiding Light." The Guiding Light of God was His Word and His promises.

Jehovah God actually gave Abraham three promises and reminded him of a fourth:

1. The promise of a great reward
2. The promise of a son to be his heir
3. The promise of his descendants being as numerous as the stars

4. And God reminded him of an earlier promise: the promise of possessing the land as an inheritance.

God was actually calling Abraham to rise above family sin and family mess.

Praise God that one day when we were bound in the family mess of our family tree, God provided The Guiding Light of the Gospel of Jesus Christ! If you have accepted Jesus Christ as your personal Savior, you have accepted the call of God to rise above family mess. If you have not accepted Jesus Christ as your personal Savior, you still can!

God does not want us to be bound by family mess. God does not want us bound by the sins of our fathers. We are bound by the sins of our fathers as a result of Adam's sin, Satan's lies, and our own depravity. But God wants to deliver us from family mess and in so doing, bring glory to His holy name. God wants us to rise above family mess.

God wanted Abraham to rise above family sin and family mess, too. But to do so Abraham would have to obey God in three areas:

1. He would have to leave his country.
2. He would have to leave his relatives.
3. He would have to leave his father's house.

If we are going to rise above our own family mess and become the men and women that God wants us to become, we are going to have to first obey God. There are no exceptions. There are no exemptions or shortcuts. Not only are we going to have to obey God if we are going to rise above family mess, but we are going to have to obey God in the same three areas. Let's look at these areas a little more closely.

If Abraham was going to rise above family mess and obey God, he was going to have to leave his country. This meant leaving a very familiar place for a place that was totally unfamiliar, because God would not reveal the place of his destination until after he left home. If Abraham was going to pull this off, he would have to have faith in God. He would have to trust God.

We have come to look at faith as intellectual assent to ideas or concepts, but faith in the Bible is trust in God. Abraham's faith required a trust in God that would allow him to abandon himself to and rest in God's promises. He would only be able to do this if he trusted the character of Jehovah God.

If we are going to rise above family mess and obey God, we are going to have to trust God. Faith is our abandonment to and rest in God's promises. God will not fully reveal His destiny for us until we leave home.

Now maybe you're saying, "I've already left home." Don't be so quick. You haven't left home if every time your mother says something it upsets you for the rest of the week. You're still at home. You haven't left home if your father's still got you all messed up. Even if your parents are dead you may still be at home. If they're still messing you up from beyond the grave, you have not left home.

- *God promised to love us with an everlasting love.* Sometimes this world can batter me and I can even begin to think that God has removed His love from me. But faith is abandonment to and rest in His promise.

- *God promised that He would never let us be tempted beyond what we are able to bear.* I know we can always look back at the end of our trial and say that He didn't put too much on us. But in the middle, it's not always so clear. But faith is abandonment to and rest in that promise.

- *God promised to conform us to the image of His dear Son.* There are times in the Christian life when the sun seems to be blotted out. I know it's back there but I can't see it and I can't feel the warmth. Faith is abandonment to and rest in God's promise.

- *God promised that He would never leave us or forsake us.* There are times when He seems to be hiding, but I choose to believe that He is still there. Faith is abandonment to and rest in that promise.

- *God promised to come back to get us one day.* I look around me and I can't find any hint that He's about to return. But He said He is, so that settles it. Faith is abandonment to and rest in that promise.

If Abraham was going to rise above family mess and become the man that God wanted him to become by obeying and trusting God, he was going to have to leave home.

Abraham was no doubt living in his father's tents. This was not unusual for the nomadic people of those times. But God wanted to do something new with Abraham. He wanted Abraham to leave his father's house and leave all his relatives. He knew that Abraham would never escape the influence of family mess as long as he lived in such close proximity to it. God had a vision for Abraham's life, but Abraham would have to accept that vision by obeying and trusting Him.

God wants to do something miraculous in the lives of every one of His children. He has a destiny for each one of us. But in order to receive the miracle and destiny of God, we must leave home.

- We must get finished with our "mother issues."
- We must tear down our father's altars.
- We must leave home volitionally, physically, intellectually, emotionally, and spiritually.
- We must leave home with all of its issues and press on towards the mark of the prize of the high calling of God in Christ Jesus.

God has a vision for our lives. To release that vision, we must accept God's vision of us—no matter how we look in our own eyes or in someone else's eyes.

We now have a glimpse of the family sin that was impacting Abraham and the call of God upon his life, but in the passage of Scripture that we are considering we see where the family mess got started. It started when Abraham partially obeyed God.

When you read Stephen's Sermon in Acts seven you can get the idea that Abraham had a hard time leaving his country and his father's home. It seems that he didn't actually leave until after his father died. This reminds me of Isaiah six: "In the year that King Uzziah died, I saw the Lord" (Isaiah 6:1a, NIV). Some of us won't see the Lord until our relatives get out of our way. This could mean that Abraham didn't obey God's Word immediately. While this is speculation, his disobedience in the situation with Lot is clear. It is hard to say exactly what happened, but his nephew, Lot, went with him. The Bible gives two perspectives:

1. It says that Lot *went with* him.
2. It also says that Abraham *took* Lot with him.

The Hebrew word for *took* can also mean *accept*, so it's hard to say. But it seems that Lot wanted to go with Abraham, and Abraham didn't have the heart to tell him, "You can't go with me, because that is God's Word." In the words of today's pop psychology, Abraham was codependent or dysfunctional. He couldn't say *no* to Lot. He couldn't set the proper boundaries where Lot was concerned.

But the problem was much larger than that. Abraham only partially obeyed God. Abraham, one of the major New Testament examples of faith, demonstrated from the beginning that he had trouble trusting God. This is important in understanding how Abraham came to be a great example of faith. His faith did not flow from his natural self but from the transforming power of the Holy Spirit.

Why did Abraham have so much trouble trusting God? I think the answer lies in his family sin. Abraham had come from a house and a country where false gods were worshiped. He was now learning to have a relationship with the true and living God. Trusting God would be a problem for Abraham over the course of his life, but God would eventually transform him into a shining example of faith. God had a vision and plan for Abraham, and not even family sin could thwart that plan—if Abraham would trust and obey.

God wanted to use Abraham, but He would first have to separate Abraham from his relatives. When Abraham allowed Lot to go with him, he allowed family mess to travel along.

Family mess will get started in our lives if we choose not to obey God because of another family member.

- We don't know how to set boundaries.
- We don't know how to say *no* to someone we love.
- We don't know how to obey God because of a difficult situation with a relative.

I wouldn't have a church now if I hadn't learned how to say *no*, at certain points, to people who were close to me. Not "No, I don't care." Not "No, I don't want to be bothered with you." But "No, this is not the will of God. I must follow God's will. I cannot do what you want me to do. I don't care how good it looks, how much it seems it will straighten out the problem, how it seems that it'll all work out. If I don't do what God tells me to do, we're going to have a serious problem. So, I must say *no.*"

If you're a married man, have you ever had to say *no* to your wife? Have you ever had God telling you one thing and your wife telling you something else? Abraham had a hard time with that. His wife was telling him one thing, and he was going to do what his wife said. Adam had a hard time with that, too. I think most men have a hard time with that.

If you're a married woman, have you ever had to say *no* when your husband's telling you, "I want you to do this" but God's saying, "I want you to do something else"? There are situations in life when we've got to say *no.* But it's very difficult, isn't it? We have to learn to chop the wood and let the chips fall where they may.

When I was growing up, I attended Shelton Temple Church of God in Christ, pastored by Bishop Olethus E. Shelton. Bishop Shelton once gave me some words of advice that I shall never forget. After some discussion about a difficult decision, he said to me, "Brother Joey, what do you want to be, a woodchopper or a chip-gatherer?" As a teenage lad, I didn't fully understand what he was asking. Nevertheless, I knew enough to know that I wanted to be a woodchopper. I said, "A woodchopper, I guess." He said, "Then chop the wood and let the chips fall where they may!"

You can't be a woodchopper and a chip-gatherer at the same time.
You either have to chop the wood and forget about the chips or
you can try to keep the chips from flying and never chop the
wood.

There are times in family relationships where we need to chop
the wood of God and let the chips fall where they may. But
most of us often try to keep the chips from flying and hitting
our relatives. We try to obey God and please relatives at the
same time. Sometimes that is impossible.

I've decided I want to be a woodchopper for Jesus Christ. I'm
going to chop the wood by faith. I'm going to obey God by faith.
I'm going to chop God's wood and let the chips of circumstances,
misunderstanding, and criticism fall where they may. God is in
control and He will take care of the location of the chips.

But we often try to keep chips from hitting our relatives. And
often, when we do, we still end up with trouble with our
relatives—and the wood of God unchopped.

There are times in our lives when God calls us to grow up
emotionally and spiritually. There are times when God calls us
to go out with Him and leave our relatives behind. You may
even need to let your children go, because you're letting them
travel with you and bring along their family mess. It is through
an intimate relationship with the Lord that He wants to begin
to deliver you from family mess. When we let our relatives travel
with us, against the direct commandments of God, we allow
family mess to travel with us and we can never get free.

God's got a wonderful purpose, plan, and vision for your life, but it may mean separation from your relatives and their family mess. What do you want to be—a woodchopper or a chip-gatherer?

DISCUSSION QUESTIONS

1. How is your own unique flavor of human depravity expressing itself in family mess in your life?

2. Compare God's vision for your life with your own vision of yourself.

3. Can you identify any relative or friend who God may be trying to separate you from emotionally?

4. How are you doing with the obedience and trust necessary to chop the wood?

5. What chips might you be trying to gather up with reference to a relative?

CHAPTER 3

The Separation of Abraham and Lot
(As the World Turns, Part 2)

Family mess happens, even as the world turns. In the previous chapter, we saw the beginning of family mess in the family of Abraham, when he allowed Lot to travel with him against the expressed Word of God, the guiding light. Now let's follow the unfolding of family mess in Abraham's family.

> So Abram went up from Egypt to the Negev, he and his wife and all that belonged to him, and Lot with him. Now Abram was very rich in livestock, in silver and in gold.
>
> He went on his journeys from the Negev as far as Bethel, to the place where his tent had been at the beginning, between Bethel and Ai, to the place of the altar which he had made there formerly; and there Abram called on the name of the LORD. Now Lot, who went with Abram, also had flocks and herds and tents. And the land could not sustain them while dwelling together, for their

possessions were so great that they were not able to remain together. And there was strife between the herdsmen of Abram's livestock and the herdsmen of Lot's livestock. Now the Canaanite and the Perizzite were dwelling then in the land. So Abram said to Lot, "Please let there be no strife between you and me, nor between my herdsmen and your herdsmen, for we are brothers. Is not the whole land before you? Please separate from me; if to the left, then I will go to the right; or if to the right, then I will go to the left."

Lot lifted up his eyes and saw all the valley of the Jordan, that it was well watered everywhere—this was before the LORD destroyed Sodom and Gomorrah—like the garden of the LORD, like the land of Egypt as you go to Zoar. So Lot chose for himself all the valley of the Jordan, and Lot journeyed eastward. Thus they separated from each other. Abram settled in the land of Canaan, while Lot settled in the cities of the valley, and moved his tents as far as Sodom. Now the men of Sodom were wicked exceedingly and sinners against the LORD.

The LORD said to Abram, after Lot had separated from him, "Now lift up your eyes and look from the place where you are, northward and southward and eastward and westward; for all the land which you see, I will give it to you and to your descendants forever. I will make your descendants as the dust of the earth, so that if anyone can number the dust of the earth, then your descendants can also be numbered. Arise, walk about the land through its length and breadth; for I will give it to you."

Then Abram moved his tent and came and dwelt by the oaks of Mamre, which are in Hebron, and there he built an altar to the LORD (Genesis 13:1–18).

We receive a great deal of important information in the phrase, *"and Lot with him."* We learn that Abraham partially obeyed God. We learn that Abraham was codependent or dysfunctional. Codependency is when you are unable to live your life except through the life of somebody else. Some people don't like to use psychological terms, so let me say it biblically: Abraham sinned. He couldn't say *no* to Lot. He couldn't set the proper boundaries where Lot was concerned.

Isn't that where a great deal of our problems start? When we fail to obey God with respect to separation from a family member? God has a special mission for every one of His children, but He often separates us unto Himself to prepare us for that mission.

This principle of *separation for preparation* is seen in numerous places in the Bible. Let's just note three:

- *God prepared Moses on the backside of the desert.* Separated from all of humanity, God manifested Himself to Moses and commissioned him to lead the Children of Israel out of Egypt.

- *God prepared Jesus in the wilderness.* After forty days of temptation in the wilderness, Jesus was ready to begin His public ministry.

- *God separated John to the Isle of Patmos.* There on Patmos, God gave John the Revelation of the end times.

Before God can use us, sometimes He has to separate us unto Himself to prepare us for service. Some people can't handle being alone. They turn on the TV or the radio or go out into public just to not feel alone. But how can God deal with us if He can never get us alone to Himself?

Remember when you were dating? When you date somebody you want to get him or her all alone, right? You don't want brothers and sisters or mother and father or anybody to come along with you—you want this special person all to yourself. God wants you all to Himself, too.

But sometimes when God wants to separate us unto Himself we try to take family members with us, family members whom God has asked us to emotionally separate from.

Though I have touched on the reason for the separation of Lot from Abraham, I think there is still a lingering note of wonder as to why God wouldn't allow Lot to remain with Abraham. There are probably many reasons, but I think the major one is that Lot represented a link to Abraham's family, whom we suspect worshiped idols.

The same is true of us. It is likely that God may want to separate you emotionally from family members that represent a link to your codependent, dysfunctional, idolatrous family systems, along with family-of-origin issues.

That is certainly a deep reason for such a separation, but the problem is much deeper than that. God wanted Abraham, a future example of faith and trust in God, to place his full trust in Him. Yet Abraham had trouble trusting Jehovah God. God knew that Abraham's codependency and inability to trust Him would lead to more family mess. God needed to separate Lot from Abraham so that He could build Abraham into the faithful, obedient servant who would one day receive a fantastic destiny.

God knows that our codependency and inability to trust Him will lead to more family mess and block His plans to make of us what He wants us to be and to give us a fantastic destiny. Therefore, sometimes He has to separate us from a family member who has a toxic effect upon us.

Over and over in the Bible we come face-to-face with two major prerequisites to a vibrant, Spirit-filled, successful life: faith and obedience. Trust and obey! Salvation is through trust and we

walk by faith or trust. And obedience is one of the greatest
demands in the Bible, because obedience highlights the
authority of Jehovah God.

In Genesis thirteen we see a report on Abraham's journey. Just
before, in the previous chapter, the Lord had told him this:

> "Go forth from your country, and from your
> relatives and from your father's house, to the land
> which I will show you; and I will make you a great
> nation, and I will bless you, and make your name
> great; and so you shall be a blessing; and I will
> bless those who bless you, and the one who curses
> you I will curse. And in you all the families of the
> earth will be blessed" (Genesis 12:1–3).

Abraham was exchanging:

- his country for the Promised Land;
- his natural relatives for God-given relatives; and
- his father's house for the house of his heavenly
  Father.

But, this was all dependent upon Abraham's faith or trust in
Jehovah God. Here are three applications of this truth:

> 1. *God wants us to exchange our father's country for the
> Promised Land of abundant Christian living.* Our
> father's country is a land of bondage to idols, but the
> Promised Land is a land where we are free to worship

the true and living God. God wants us to exchange bondage for freedom, a fleshly walk for a Spirit-filled walk, and punishment for reward.

2. *God wants us to exchange our relatives for the family of God.* He wants us to give up our Adamic family for the body of Jesus Christ. We don't have to treat them badly or refuse to talk to people in our natural, human family, but they cannot get between us and the wood-chopping that God has assigned to our hands.

3. *God wants us to exchange faith in our natural fathers and ancestry for faith in Him as our heavenly Father and our heavenly ancestry.* Paul's words capture this point beautifully: *"For we are the true circumcision, who worship in the Spirit of God and glory in Christ Jesus and **put no confidence in the flesh**"* (Philippians 3:3, emphasis mine). Our confidence is in Jesus Christ, not the flesh, neither ours nor that of our family members.

As Abraham continued his sojourn, he came upon the place where he had previously built an altar. There he began to call upon the name of the Lord. Abraham had a custom of building an altar every time He encountered God or something of great spiritual significance occurred. These altars were for memorialization and worship. Every time Abraham would come across one of his altars, he was reminded of what God had done for him and inspired to worship God afresh.

Likewise, we too need to build worship markers in our lives to remember and celebrate a fresh encounter with or blessing of

Jehovah God. When we see the marker and are reminded of what God did, we should call upon His name and worship Him afresh.

Now we come to the expression of the family mess that Abraham facilitated by allowing Lot to travel along with him. As Abraham journeyed toward the Promised Land, Abraham's herdsmen and Lot's herdsmen began quarreling. As the world turns, family mess happens! Abraham and Lot were both rich. They both had a great deal of livestock, and the land could not support both herds. Had Abraham trusted and obeyed God, he would not have let Lot travel with him and would have avoided this whole family mess.

Oh, what mess Abraham brought upon himself and his family when he chose to distrust and disobey God! No, this was not the blatant sin of commission, but the sin of omission. It's not so much what Abraham did that got them all in trouble, but what he did not do. Abraham disobeyed God by failing to do what He wanted him to do.

We can be like that, too, can't we? Sometimes we sit in places where we ought to be doing something, but we do nothing. We're passive. In being passive, we end up letting the will of God not be done. That's a sin of omission. Oh, what family mess we bring upon ourselves when we choose to distrust and disobey God! We bring great pain and misery into our lives through negligence and through sins of omission, particularly when we fail to set boundaries with our family members.

Now Abraham is faced with trying to solve this mess with Lot. He stated his values to Lot and said that they should not be fighting because they were relatives. Then Abraham, not wanting to be involved in family mess, offered Lot a solution. He said, in effect, "Go wherever you want to go. Take the best land, if you want, and I will take whatever's left." Abraham was willing to experience loss so that there might be peace between himself and his relative.

Is this a good thing or a bad thing? Abraham's offer may be a manifestation of both biblical values and Abraham's passivity. I'm going to take up the subject of Abraham's passivity in a later chapter, so right now let's consider the biblical values that Abraham displayed in this situation.

The biblical values that I see are love, peace, and personal sacrifice. These are certainly principles that we should seek to emulate and practice in our lives. We should love others, particularly family members. We should consider others as better than ourselves. And we should be willing to suffer loss for the sake of peace.

As I pointed out in chapter one, although family mess is very painful and destructive, it can alert us to areas of struggle or sin where God wants to work. Abraham struggled in trusting Jehovah God. This family mess with Lot gave Abraham an opportunity to learn to trust in God and manifest that trust through obedience and love.

Likewise, God often uses family mess as an opportunity for us to live out and demonstrate our Christianity. So when we see family mess starting to happen, we should start looking for a personal area of struggle and how God wants to work on us, in us, and through us.

When you see family mess happening in your family—and as the world turns, it will happen—start looking for a way that you can let the light of Jesus Christ shine through you. When you see at the family reunion that Aunt So & So isn't talking to Cousin Such & Such, it's an opportunity for ministry. It's an opportunity for the lost members of your family to see that there is something different about you, and the difference is Jesus.

When you're at the funeral and they start to fight over Daddy's stuff, it's time to show the difference between you and them. When you are at the wedding rehearsal and they can't find the groom, it's a time that you ought to intercede in family mess and show the difference between you and them. So, the next time you see family mess, instead of running, ask, "How can God use me in this? How can I be what God wants me to be in this? What is God saying to me in this?"

This episode in Abraham's life gives us a much better perspective of why Abraham and Lot needed to be separated: They did not have the same value system and they were not looking for the same things. Abraham's value system was more others-oriented. Lot's value system was more self-oriented. Abraham was looking for a city whose architect and builder was God. Lot was looking for something far different.

We see here what Lot was looking for. Lot lifted up his eyes and saw the valley of Jordan. It was well-watered like the Garden of Eden, but it was in the direction of Sodom and Gomorrah. It was farther eastward. It was in the direction where the rest of the world was traveling. He selfishly chose the direction of the world.

When Adam and Eve were expelled from the Garden of Eden, they were expelled to the east:

> So He drove the man out; and at the east of the garden of Eden He stationed the cherubim and the flaming sword which turned every direction to guard the way to the tree of life (Genesis 3:24).

Not only were Adam and Eve expelled to the east of Eden, but it seems that their offspring and all of mankind were moving to the east:

— *"Then Cain went out from the presence of the* Lord, *and settled in the land of Nod, east of Eden"* (Genesis 4:16).

— *"It came about as they journeyed east, that they found a plain in the land of Shinar and settled there"* (Genesis 11:2).

— *"Then he proceeded from there to the mountain on the east of Bethel, and pitched his tent, with Bethel on the west and Ai on the east; and there he built an altar*

to the LORD and called upon the name of the LORD"
(Genesis 12:8).

— "So Lot chose for himself all the valley of the Jordan,
and Lot journeyed eastward. Thus they separated from
each other" (Genesis 13:11).

Thus, the whole world was traveling east. East represents the
way of the world. All that is in the world is the lust of the flesh,
the lust of the eyes, and the boastful pride of life. All of these
were probably operating when Lot chose the well-watered land
towards the valley of Jordan. So, while Abraham was looking
for a city whose Builder and Maker was God, Lot was looking
for the world.

Now we can see the fact that while Lot goes farther east,
Abraham goes west. *Abraham appears to be the first man to
choose to go in an opposite direction from the world.* He is the
first man to eschew the secular, conventional direction and
wisdom and go in the direction of the Lord.

If we are going to be used by God, there are times when we
must choose to go the opposite way from the direction everyone
we know is going. I have faced this situation many times, and
will face it many times more if the Lord should delay His
coming.

Now we come to a very important principle: God used family
mess to separate Lot from Abraham and cause Abraham to go
in the direction He wanted. As painful, frustrating, and

devastating as family mess can be, God often uses it to separate us from dysfunctional relatives and causes us to go in the direction He wants us to go!

Now I ask you: Are there family members that God wants to separate you from? Are there relationships that God wants to separate you from? Not necessarily because of sin, but because God wants to do something great with you and through you—something that He cannot do while you are still mixed up with worldly relatives.

If you won't obey God and voluntarily separate from those relatives, God may use family mess to do the job. There is a price for being used by God. It will cost you some separation, some isolation, and some pain.

Now, after God separates Lot from Abraham, He begins to speak to Abraham. God reveals to Abraham the land that He was promising to him. He tells Abraham to look northward, southward, eastward, and westward. He says, *"All the land which you see, I will give it to you and to your descendants forever"* (Genesis 13:15). He told him to walk through the land, because He was going to give it to him.

After Lot is separated from Abraham, it seems that God kicks His program into high gear. What can we learn from this?

- God could not or would not talk to Abraham until Abraham trusted Him.

- God could not or would not talk to Abraham until Abraham obeyed Him.

- God could not or would not talk to Abraham until He separated him from Lot unto Himself.

- God could not or would not reaffirm His promises to Abraham until he was separated unto Himself.

How does this apply to you?

- Sometimes God cannot or will not speak to you because you have not trusted Him.

- Sometimes God cannot or will not speak to you because you have not obeyed Him.

- Sometimes God cannot or will not speak to you because you have not separated yourself from dysfunctional family members.

After God has separated you unto Himself from worldly relatives, He can give you the promises that He wants you to consider. This is great news: God is able to work through and beyond family mess to give you His blessed promises. Hallelujah!

There is only one more thing that we need to know: How do we receive the promises of God? The Bible tells us that Abraham traveled a little bit farther, and when he set up his tent he built another altar to the Lord. Every time God did something significant for Abraham, he built an altar and worshiped the Lord. Abraham accepted God's promises through worship. The only way to accept God's promises is through worship. Once God uses family mess to separate us to Himself and He reaffirms His promises to us, the only proper response is worship.

DISCUSSION QUESTIONS

1. How has the principle of *separation for preparation* come into play in your life?

2. What does your trust and obedience of Jehovah God look like at this point in your journey?

3. How are you responding to relatives who God may be separating you from?

4. Which way are you traveling in your life: the way of the world or the way of the Lord? How do you know?

5. How is your altar building coming? Recall some previous worship markers that you have set up, and worship God afresh!

CHAPTER 4

How To Serve Separated Family Members

We are beginning to see that family mess has a long-term impact upon the members of the family. In this chapter, we continue to explore that long-term impact.

In the last chapter we saw that Lot's choice of the well-watered valley of Jordan in the vicinity of Sodom and Gomorrah was a selfish choice that was based on following the direction of the world. In this chapter we'll see how Lot's choice affected his immediate family. We're going to see some generational bondage and some additional reasons why God separated Lot from Abraham. And we are also going to see how God continued to work in the life of Lot, beyond the family mess.

The background information to this story is very long, so I will not print the entire Scripture text here. I have chosen to summarize the story in my own words. Nevertheless, you may want to read the eighteenth and nineteenth chapters of Genesis before you move into the rest of this chapter.

In the eighteenth chapter of Genesis, we read that the Lord appeared to Abraham while he was sitting at the door of his tent during the heat of the day. As he lifted up his eyes, he saw three men approaching. We now know that one of the men was God. This was a pre-Bethlehem appearance of our Lord and Savior, Jesus Christ. We can also speculate that the other two men were angels.

Abraham arose to extend the customary Near Eastern hospitality. He prepared a meal for them, and they ate it. As they ate, they asked, "Where is your wife, Sarah?" Then one of them prophesied, "At this time next year, your wife shall have a son." Sarah was listening to the men talk. Since she and Abraham were old and she was past the age of childbearing, she laughed to herself.

The Lord heard her and asked Sarah, "Why did you laugh? Is anything too difficult for the Lord?" Sarah denied that she had laughed because she was afraid. The Lord then reaffirmed His prophecy concerning a son for Abraham and Sarah at the same time next year.

Now the men rose and started walking in the direction of Sodom, and Abraham was walking with them to see them off. Then we come to one of those enigmatic passages of Scripture. The Lord said, "Shall I hide what I am about to do from Abraham, since I have a completely different and great destiny for him?"

We don't know who the Lord is talking to, since that is not stated. He seems to be talking to the other two angels or to Himself. But that is the enigmatic thing about this narrative: Why would God be asking Himself such a question? God knows all things, right? God already knows everything that He is going to do, right? This is simply an anthropomorphism (attributing human characteristics to God), right? Well, that is a subject for another book.

Whomever God was talking to, it appears He was considering hiding His intentions from Abraham because Sodom was where Lot, Abraham's nephew, lived. Perhaps He didn't want Abraham to be hurt or sidetracked. But, it seems that the Lord decided to share with Abraham what He was about to do. He said:

> "The outcry of Sodom and Gomorrah is indeed great, and their sin is exceedingly grave. I will go down now, and see if they have done entirely according to its outcry, which has come to Me; and if not, I will know" (Genesis 18:20–21).

It seems that God wanted to thoroughly examine the extent of their sin. Once again this does not fit with our concept of God. But that simply means that our concept of God is obviously not completely right.

So, the Lord stood in His place, while the two men went towards Sodom. Now Abraham, understanding what was taking place, approached the Lord and began to bargain for the lives of the people of Sodom, and consequently, Lot and his family.

There is a wonderful lesson here. Even though God had separated Lot from Abraham and God had a tremendous destiny for Abraham, Abraham was still concerned about Lot—and rightly so. He could not demonstrate that concern by disobeying God and living with Lot, but He could demonstrate it by interceding for Lot.

In the last chapter, we studied how God often separates us from sinful, dysfunctional relatives so that He might guide us to our destiny. But now we see how we should respond to separated relatives. We don't dislike them or think we are better than them or forget about them, because, but for the grace of God, we would be looking at ourselves. No, we intercede with God on their behalf. We pray for them while they are down in Sodom and Gomorrah.

Now, I have a question for you: Do you have any relatives down in Sodom and Gomorrah? Where is Sodom and Gomorrah? It's on the streets. It's down as deep and as low and as far as you can go. It's the last stop before hell. This is way down, even farther than the prodigal son went. This is way out in Sodom and Gomorrah. Do you have any relatives out there?

Grandfather, grandmother, father, mother, brother, sister, aunt, or uncle—keep on praying for your relatives until God delivers them from Sodom. Perhaps you have a relative who is a long way from the tents and altars of Abraham—don't stop praying for him until you see him making his way out of Sodom and Gomorrah.

Let's look at Abraham's prayer and see what we can learn. As Abraham prayed to God, he began to play on God's justice by asking this question: *"Will You indeed sweep away the righteous with the wicked?"* (Genesis 18:23b). In other words, "You're too just to sweep away the righteous with the wicked! You're too just to exact the penalty for sinning upon innocent people." Then Abraham began to bargain for the lives of the people of Sodom, and his nephew Lot. He asked God:

> "Suppose there are fifty righteous within the city; will You indeed sweep it away and not spare the place for the sake of the fifty righteous who are in it? Far be it from You to do such a thing, to slay the righteous with the wicked, so that the righteous and the wicked are treated alike. Far be it from You! Shall not the Judge of all the earth deal justly?"
>
> So the LORD said, "If I find in Sodom fifty righteous within the city, then I will spare the whole place on their account" (Genesis 18:24–26).

It seems, at this point, that Abraham realized he was on shaky ground in two areas:

1. *He, being nothing but dust and ashes, had ventured to speak to God on this matter.* Abraham had something we don't have today: It's called reverence. He understood to Whom he was talking. Modern people

don't understand to whom they are talking when they talk to God. I've heard people say, "Well, you know, I'm not afraid of God." And I just start backing up, because when the ground opens up under them I don't want to be standing too close. God is an awesome God and He's not to be toyed with. But we don't seem to reverence anyone or anything anymore.

2. *He had used a figure that was too high.* So Abraham began to lower his number, and Abraham and God continued to bargain back and forth. What about forty-five? What about forty? What about thirty or twenty or ten? And God said, "I will not destroy it on account of the ten." When he finished bargaining, the Lord departed and Abraham went back to his camp.

In the nineteenth chapter of Genesis, the story shifts from Abraham and the Lord to the two men who accompanied the Lord. Our previous speculation on the identity of these two men is confirmed: Genesis 19:1 calls them angels. As these two angels approached Sodom in the evening, Lot was sitting in the gate. This implies that Lot was evidently an important man and a leader in Sodom, since the city gates were where the leaders would sit to govern Near Eastern cities.

When Lot saw the two angels he—as his Uncle Abraham had done—extended to them the customary greetings and hospitality of that time. He invited them to stay with him for the night. The angels wanted to stay in the town square, but Lot strongly urged them to stay with him, and he prepared a feast for them.

Before Lot and his guests retired for the evening, the men of Sodom surrounded Lot's house and demanded that he bring out the two men so that they could have homosexual relations with them.

Now we begin to get a picture of the city that Lot had chosen for a home. Remember, Lot chose to go the way of the world when he chose to live there. We also get a glimpse of what the Lord meant when He said that the sin of Sodom was exceedingly grave. Did you know that we get the word *sodomy* from this story about Sodom? Homosexuality is, according to God's Word, an abomination in His sight.

Lot, feeling some responsibility for his guests, offered these wicked men his two daughters instead of his guests. This seems strange to us but may actually have been considered the height of politeness in Lot's culture. Even so, Lot's Middle Eastern morality and sensibilities were not to be substituted for the protection of Jehovah God. So perhaps we get a glimpse of one reason why God was separating Lot from Abraham.

> But they said, "Stand aside." Furthermore, they said, "This one came in as an alien, and already he is acting like a judge; now we will treat you worse than them." So they pressed hard against Lot and came near to break the door (Genesis 19:9).

At this point, the two angels pulled Lot into the house, shut the door, and smote the men with blindness, so that they had trouble finding the door.

Then the angels asked Lot, "Who else do you have in this city? You'd better get them to your house quick, because we're about to destroy this city." This was as serious as it gets. So Lot went to plead with his sons-in-law, but to them he appeared to be jesting. Isn't this the same today? We are concerned about the destruction that will take place at the Second Coming of the Lord, so we go to our relatives to warn them, but they think we are jesting!

Remember all of this is happening to Lot because of his own choices: (1) to leave with Abraham and (2) to dwell in Sodom and Gomorrah. So often we blame the world or the devil or even God for our problems, when all the time it is our own choices that have brought us to trouble.

When the morning dawned the angels told Lot to take his wife and two daughters and flee because they were going to destroy the city. Remember, God had agreed to spare the city if ten righteous people could be found in it. But Lot could only come up with four.

It's interesting to me that Peter called Lot *righteous* even though living in Sodom had negatively impacted his values and morality (see 2 Peter 2:7). I believe this is where a number of Christian people are: They are righteous, meaning they have received the imputed righteousness of Jesus Christ and are attempting to live righteous lives according to the power of the Holy Spirit, but they have been greatly impacted by the evil of the American culture. They don't even realize how much they have been impacted. Many of us don't realize how deeply we have been influenced by the American culture. Please notice with me the following:

- *We have little passion for the things of God.* If we were passionate about godly things, we would be on fire about reading His Word, praying, going to church, witnessing, and obeying God. But so much of the time we just go through the motions.

- *We have little commitment.* Any old thing will knock us out. "I don't like the way they seated me last Sunday, so I'm not going back." "I don't like the songs they sang last time—I'm not going to go back."

- *We have little submission to either God's direct authority or His delegated authority.* There is no authority over you except what has been established by God. Your husband is a delegated authority. Your mother and father are a delegated authority. The state is a delegated authority. Your pastor is a delegated authority.

- *We have a hard time hearing the voice of God.* People say to me, "I just can't hear God's voice; would you help me make this decision?" You're not going to hear His voice if you don't come to church, read His Word, fellowship with Christians, or pray. Where are you going to hear His voice? You're not.

- *We are burned out when we ought to be energized by the power of the Holy Spirit.* Most of the folks I know are burned out. Some need to be burned up! But many are burned out and can't get anything, don't know anything, can hardly go on, and can hardly make it. We ought to be empowered by God's Spirit.

Okay, back to the story. When the angels warned Lot to flee, he and his family hesitated. That's understandable. All they owned and almost everyone they knew were about to be destroyed. But there's another possible explanation for their hesitancy: It's possible that they didn't want to leave Sodom because of their attachment to the secularization and sin of the city. God used family mess to get Lot away from Abraham, but He would have to use tragedy to get Lot away from his worldly associations.

God is saying to us, "I want to bless you and give you a destiny, but you will have to leave the comfort, association, and trust in your favorite relatives and you will have to leave your worldly associations and possessions behind."

When Lot and his family hesitated, the angels seized their hands and led them outside of the city, because *God's compassion was upon Lot.* God's compassion was upon Lot even in the midst of family mess and tragedy. God's compassion is upon you, too, even in the midst of family mess and tragedy. This is a great reason to thank and praise God!

Over in Peter's second letter, he used this situation with Lot to state the truth that God knows how to rescue the godly from temptation. Just as God knew how to rescue Lot from Sodom, where he was oppressed by the sensual conduct of unprincipled men, and his soul was tormented by their lawless deeds, He knows how to deliver you from similar ungodly situations, even if He has to use tragedy.

After the angels led Lot and his family out of the city, one of them gave this warning: *"Escape for your life! Do not look behind you, and do not stay anywhere in the valley; escape to the mountains, or you will be swept away"* (Genesis 19:17).

You would think by now, after all that he had seen, Lot would have been running away from Sodom as fast as he could. But he wasn't. Instead, Lot pleads with the angels to let him escape to the little town of Zoar. It seems that he could not bear being too far away from Sodom. He seems to be saying, "I can't live in the mountains, far away from Sodom. Let me flee to this little town instead." His life is wrapped up with the whole region of Sodom.

Well, the angels granted his request and urged his speedy escape because they could not do anything until he was a safe distance from the coming destruction.

Oh, the truth here is rich! Lot represents those of us who are righteous, but worldly or carnal. John wrote:

> Do not love the world nor the things in the world.
> If anyone loves the world, the love of the Father
> is not in him. For all that is in the world, the lust
> of the flesh and the lust of the eyes and the
> boastful pride of life, is not from the Father, but
> is from the world. The world is passing away, and
> also its lusts; but the one who does the will of
> God lives forever (1 John 2:15–17).

Many times we are just like Lot. God wants to separate us from
the world, which in many cases torments us. Yet in spite of the
torment we may feel, we are often so wrapped up, tangled up,
and tied up with the world that we feel we cannot live without
it. We don't believe we can live without the secular associations
and possessions of this world. I think of worldly friends, TV,
movies, and questionable amusements like nightclubs. God is
telling us to flee for our lives, but we are still hanging around.

Let's talk about television. Do you doubt that television is full
of godlessness? Sometimes God wants us to put it away for a
while—maybe a day, maybe a week, maybe forever. You'd think
that when people get saved they'd be running for their lives
from godless things like we see on TV. God is saying, "Flee for
your life, run!" And, we're saying, "I want to run, but could I
just see my favorite program before I leave?"

What about movies? There are some bastions of holiness in
this country that don't allow people on their board to go to
movies. Now I'm not saying that's right or wrong, I'm saying
that's a standard. Where are our standards today? We'll watch

anything and then wonder why we are the way we are. And God is telling us, "Flee for your life!"

We are not only tormented, but also tempted, and God wants to deliver us from both. So God sends His angels to lead us *by the hand* out of temptation. But still, even after He has led us out, we stand around and ask God if we can remain close to the secular, sinful lifestyle that we have grown accustomed to. God, being the compassionate God that He is, will often grant our requests. But there is a price to pay.

When Lot reached Zoar, the Lord rained fire and brimstone on Sodom and Gomorrah. The word "brimstone" seems to mean burning sulfur. I am told that sulfur is one of the components in the remains of a nuclear blast. All of this indicates that God destroyed Sodom and Gomorrah with fire and tremendous heat. He destroyed the people and the vegetation.

One day God is going to begin His urban renewal project on earth. Notice this passage of Scripture:

> But the day of the Lord will come like a thief, in which the heavens will pass away with a roar and the elements will be destroyed with intense heat, and the earth and its works will be burned up. Since all these things are to be destroyed in this way, what sort of people ought you to be in holy conduct and godliness, looking for and hastening the coming of the day of God, because of which the heavens will be destroyed by burning, and

the elements will melt with intense heat! But according to His promise we are looking for new heavens and a new earth, in which righteousness dwells (2 Peter 3:10–13).

So it behooves us to be ready by living a life of godliness through the power of the Holy Spirit.

Right at the end of this paragraph in Genesis 19, we are given—in just one verse—some very shocking and important information about Lot's wife: *"But his wife, from behind him, looked back, and she became a pillar of salt"* (Genesis 19:26). I'll talk some more about this in the next chapter, and I'll also talk about the impact of this incident upon Lot's daughters. But for now let's wrap up what we are learning in this passage of Scripture.

Abraham rose early in the morning, as many men of God were known to do in that day, and stood in the place where he had stood before the Lord. As he stood there, Abraham looked toward Sodom and Gomorrah, and the valley where these two cities were situated, and beheld smoke rising from the land like smoke rising from a furnace. And then we clearly see Abraham's continued impact upon Lot's life. When God destroyed the cities of Sodom and Gomorrah, He remembered Abraham and sent Lot out of the midst of those cities.

- He remembered His covenant with Abraham.
- He remembered His promise and destiny for Abraham.
- He remembered Abraham's pleading and praying for Lot.

Because of one righteous man, God rescued Lot out of the midst of Sodom and Gomorrah and did not destroy him.

Even though God may have separated you from some of your relatives for a greater purpose and your fellowship with them is almost non-existent, you should not forget about them. Intercede for them through strong, persistent prayer. Plead and bargain for their lives. Perhaps God will deliver your relatives because of you.

I've seen God deliver people out of impossible situations. I've seen people a long way from home, tied up in dope, caught up with gangsters and gangs, and folks said they couldn't get out and be free. But I've seen God send angels in among violent people and grab them by the hand and lead them out.

Keep praying for your friends and relatives down in Sodom and Gomorrah because God might just deliver them on account of you.

DISCUSSION QUESTIONS

1. Can you think of any relatives whom God has separated from you who need your continued intercessory prayer?

2. Can you relate to Lot's entanglement with his culture? On a scale of 1 to 10, with 1 being no impact and 10 being totally overwhelmed, rate your present entanglement in your culture. How would you be rated by someone who knows you well?

3. Devise and share your plan to intercede for separated family members who are living in Sodom and Gomorrah.

CHAPTER 5

In the Grip of a Mother's Gaze
(One Life to Live)

The angels had just led Lot and his wife and two daughters out of Sodom. They were fleeing for their lives because God was about to destroy the wicked cities of that well-watered valley.

Let's pick up the story in Genesis 19:23–38.

> The sun had risen over the earth when Lot came to Zoar. Then the Lord rained on Sodom and Gomorrah brimstone and fire from the Lord out of heaven, and He overthrew those cities, and all the valley, and all the inhabitants of the cities, and what grew on the ground. But his wife, from behind him, looked back, and she became a pillar of salt.
>
> Now Abraham arose early in the morning and went to the place where he had stood before the Lord; and he looked down toward Sodom and

Gomorrah, and toward all the land of the valley, and he saw, and behold, the smoke of the land ascended like the smoke of a furnace.

Thus it came about, when God destroyed the cities of the valley, that God remembered Abraham, and sent Lot out of the midst of the overthrow, when He overthrew the cities in which Lot lived (Genesis 19:23–29).

When Lot and his family reached Zoar, God destroyed Sodom and Gomorrah. This is a picture of what is going to happen at the end of the world as we know it. When we, God's children, the elect of all the ages, are safe—after the rapture or translation—God is going to destroy this world with fervent heat.

This is also a picture of the cultural conditions that will exist when Jesus is revealed.

"And just as it happened in the days of Noah, so it will be also in the days of the Son of Man: they were eating, they were drinking, they were marrying, they were being given in marriage, until the day that Noah entered the ark, and the flood came and destroyed them all.

"It was the same as happened in the days of Lot: they were eating, they were drinking, they were buying, they were selling, they were planting, they were building; but on the day that Lot went out from Sodom it rained fire and brimstone from heaven and destroyed them all.

"It will be just the same on the day that the Son of Man is revealed" (Luke 17:26–30).

Are we not experiencing the same cultural conditions now?

Aren't people eating as never before? There are restaurants everywhere and more are being built. It's a drive-thru generation. Doesn't anybody cook anymore?

Aren't people drinking as never before? There are probably more beverages, alcoholic and non-alcoholic, to choose from today than there have ever been in the history of man.

Aren't people marrying and being given in marriage as never before? Marrying and divorcing and remarrying. When all those divorced people get remarried six and seven times, it makes the marriage rate go up.

Aren't people buying as never before? Consumerism is at an all-time high. For those of us who are plain, old-fashioned lazy, we do not have to go grocery shopping anymore. We can go online with our computers and order our groceries and they will bring them to our houses.

Aren't people selling as never before? Aren't fewer farmers planting more than ever before? Aren't people building as never before?

There are new expensive houses going up all around Akron, where I live. The conditions are perfect for the return of Jesus Christ!

But now we come to an editorial comment that is very important. In verse twenty-six, we come to this report: *"But his wife, from behind him, looked back, and she became a pillar of salt"* (Genesis 19:26).

We don't even get this poor woman's name, but we do get a summation of her actions and the consequences of her actions. The phrase looked back in Hebrew is *nabat*. It means "to scan or look intently at." By implication it means "to regard with pleasure, favor, or care."

Lot's wife didn't glance back casually on Sodom and Gomorrah and the destruction that was taking place. She gazed back at Sodom and Gomorrah with pleasure. She was fondly remembering a city that was totally vile, evil, corrupt, and against God. She was enamored with Sodom and did not want to leave it or to have it destroyed. She loved Sodom and Gomorrah. She loved the world. Therefore, the love of the Father was not in her.

I believe that Jesus touched on this situation in Luke's Gospel:

> Another also said, "I will follow You, Lord; but first permit me to say good-bye to those at home." But Jesus said to him, "No one, after putting his hand to the plow and looking back, is fit for the kingdom

of God." (Luke 9:61–62)

You can't plow a straight row while looking back. The only way to plow straight is to keep your eyes straight ahead. He that keeps looking back will plow crooked.

I believe Jesus is talking discipleship here. In the preceding verses He said, *"Follow Me!"* No one can plow a straight row as a disciple by longingly looking back to the past—a past life or love. Now Jesus lets us know that He is applying this metaphor to something much more important than plowing in a field. He who puts his hand to the plow and looks back is not fit for the kingdom of God. The Greek word *fit* is *euthetos,* which means "well-placed, suited for, or adapted to."

A person who intently and longingly looks back upon his past life is not adapted to or suited for kingdom life. One scholar, F. F. Bruce, said such a person is "not fitted from the perspective of inconsiderate impulse"—i.e. the impulses and passions have not been adapted to the kingdom life—"not fitted with regard to conflicting duties"— a disciple's duties are before him, towards Heaven, not behind him in the past and the world— and "not fitted for the kingdom of Heaven, from the perspective of a divided mind"—his mind is divided from the things of God and His kingdom.

Doesn't this describe many Christians today? They have placed their faith in Jesus Christ for salvation, but:

- They are looking back into the world.

- Their impulses and passions are worldly.
- They are conflicted about their duties.
- Their minds are divided.

Instead of looking to the future and the new city and destiny where God is leading, they are looking intently and longingly towards the city where they used to live. They are rehearsing with fondness the evil, vile, godless city and are lovingly remembering their past life in sin.

And what is the outcome of looking back? Lot's wife turned into a pillar of salt.

To me, Lot represents something different than his wife and family. Lot was called righteous, but no one else in his family was. And even though Lot was righteous, he had become so entangled with the culture of Sodom that he was saved on the basis of Abraham, not because of his own righteousness. Lot's family was saved because of Lot, however. If Lot's escape from Sodom was deliverance, then the escape of his wife and daughters represents salvation.

Even though Lot's wife was saved from the destruction of Sodom and Gomorrah, she was turned into a pillar of salt when she looked back. Salt is a symbol of many things in the Bible, but in this case I believe salt is a symbol of desolation and barrenness. This is sometimes the symbolism of salt, perhaps because of the barrenness of the Dead Sea, the biblical Salt Sea.

Lot's wife escaped destruction, but her life ended up in

desolation and barrenness. She had but "One Life to Live." It would have been better had she lived it for God!

It's like many of us Christians who are dead and barren because we've got an inlet but no outlet. All we do is come to church and take in, but we never let out. All we do is come to church and eat and eat, but we're not in any ministry, we're not ministering to anybody on a regular basis. Therefore we become dead, nothing can live in us, because of the barrenness—like the Dead Sea. Notice:

1. We can escape Sodom and Gomorrah and still end up desolate and barren.

2. We can escape fire and brimstone and still end up with a life that is desolate and barren of impact.

3. We can escape the lake that burns with fire and brimstone and still experience desolation and barrenness in this life, which will result in a loss of reward in the life to come, and weeping and gnashing of teeth when we see Him.

But all of this is just background for what I really want to talk about in this chapter. I want to talk about how Lot's two daughters were caught in the grip of their mother's gaze. Their mother gazed back upon Sodom and that gaze had a profound impact upon her two daughters. Soon after this, Lot's two daughters commit incest with their father that they might preserve their family line. Can you say family mess?

Lot went up from Zoar, and stayed in the mountains, and his two daughters with him; for he was afraid to stay in Zoar; and he stayed in a cave, he and his two daughters.

Then the firstborn said to the younger, "Our father is old, and there is not a man on earth to come in to us after the manner of the earth. Come, let us make our father drink wine, and let us lie with him that we may preserve our family through our father." So they made their father drink wine that night, and the firstborn went in and lay with her father; and he did not know when she lay down or when she arose.

On the following day, the firstborn said to the younger, "Behold, I lay last night with my father; let us make him drink wine tonight also; then you go in and lie with him, that we may preserve our family through our father." So they made their father drink wine that night also, and the younger arose and lay with him; and he did not know when she lay down or when she arose.

Thus both the daughters of Lot were with child by their father. The firstborn bore a son, and called his name Moab; he is the father of the Moabites to this day. As for the younger, she also bore a son, and called his name Ben-ammi; he is the father of the sons of Ammon to this day (Genesis 19:30–38).

We don't know the family mess of Lot's wife, but there must have been some, because she left a terrible legacy of it to her daughters. Something she did in her life made their sin possible, and she sealed it when she looked back at Sodom and turned into a pillar of salt. Notice:

- That look had an impact upon her daughters.

- That look probably confirmed something in her daughters.

- That look continued her daughters' entanglement into the culture and values of Sodom.

- That look taught her daughters something about what values were important.

- That look taught her daughters something about what they should love.

- That look taught her daughters something about the past.

- That look taught her daughters something about the future.

- That look taught her daughters something about sin.

- That look became a trap to her daughters.

These two daughters were trapped in the grip of the gaze of their mother.

If you are a mother, beware of your gaze! Be careful what you gaze upon, because your daughters will undoubtedly be trapped in the grip of your gaze. Up till now we've been talking about the sin of the fathers, but the Bible says the sin of the mothers impacts future generations, too. Your daughters will be in the grip of whatever you gaze on. If your gaze is toward the way of the world, that grip may manifest itself in the following ways (by the way, these work for sons, too):

1. *Gazing back at Sodom may teach your daughters to love the world rather than the things of God.* What do they see in you? What will be emblazoned into their minds about you as their mother? If they saw you gazing back with fondness, they're going to learn to love the world rather than the things of God.

2. *Gazing back at Sodom may teach your daughters to be enamored with sin rather than with holy living.* If they saw you so enamored with sin, constantly gazing back at it until you become fixed on it and your life is barren because of it, don't think that your daughters will escape that. God may save them and they may move on, but don't think that they can escape the impact of your gaze. They may even become trapped by it.

3. *Gazing back at Sodom may teach your daughters to live in the past rather than living in the present and looking toward the future.* Many people blame everything that's wrong with them on the fact that their mothers didn't give them enough milk and cookies or whatever else. You can't always look back. You've got to take responsibility for your own life and your own choices. It's time to be running for your life, not looking back at yesteryear.

4. *Gazing back at Sodom may teach your daughters to be trapped in the evil of their past.* Some people have had truly horrible things done to them in their past. If something like that happened to you, I have great compassion for you. But if you constantly look back at that you can become trapped by it and you may not deal with it, and your daughters may become trapped by it, too. They'll be trapped by that legacy of evil that happened to you and may be left trying to finish up your pain.

5. *Gazing back at Sodom may teach your daughters to love the culture rather than the principles of the Word of God.* When we're fixated on the ways of the world, we care less about the principles of God. Instead of becoming biblically astute we become politically correct. You can't talk about abortion anymore because people will get mad at you. You can't talk about divorce anymore because folks will get mad. They're looking at things from a cultural perspective, not a biblical perspective. Brother

or sister, it doesn't matter what the TV says about abortion or divorce or whatever; what matters is what the Bible says about it.

6. *Gazing back at Sodom may teach your daughters something abnormal and abominable about human sexuality.* What have your daughters seen about your own sexuality? Most of us have never seen much about our parent's sexuality because they hid it from us. And they ought to hide the actual act of intercourse, but they ought not to hide all sexuality from us. Because we can't learn what it's all about in a normal family if we don't see some of it. But what did your daughters see? Have they seen you let men stay overnight?

7. *Gazing back at Sodom may teach your daughters something perverted about their womanhood.* The reason we don't have many real, biblical women, today is that all the females are looking back at the culture to find out how to be a woman. You don't look at *Knot's Landing* to find out what a woman ought to be. You don't look at *General Hospital* to figure out what a woman is supposed to be. You look in the Word of God to find out what a woman ought to be.

8. *Gazing back at Sodom may teach your daughters something about honoring or dishonoring their parents.* Think about Lot's daughters conspiring to commit incest with him. How much honor were they showing him when they tricked their father to have sex with them,

not one time, but twice? Family mess and parental dishonor are the legacy of Lot's wife.

9. *Gazing back at Sodom may teach your daughters to have messy, sinful ideas about how to fulfill their destiny.* Again, think about Lot's daughters committing incest. What a mess. You don't fulfill your destiny by sin; you fulfill your destiny through God. They said, "We're not going to have any offspring, so we've got to do something about it." What about waiting on the Lord? They took matters into their own hands and created a big-time family mess.

"Behold, everyone who quotes proverbs will quote this proverb concerning you, saying, 'Like mother, like daughter'" (Ezekiel 16:44).

I want to wrap up this chapter with two observations:

1. In keeping with understanding the phrase *"visiting the iniquity of the fathers upon the children to the third and fourth generations,"* we have looked at the impact of family mess two generations away from Abraham. Lot was Abraham's nephew, so that is one generation away, and Lot's daughters are two generations away. So we can begin to see the impact of a father's sin upon the children in the second generation.

2. We can see that God worked beneath, behind, through, above, and beyond family mess. God worked in spite of the family mess to deliver Lot and his daughters from destruction down in Sodom.

Our God is a compassionate and powerful God, and He will work beneath, behind, through, above, beyond, and in spite of family mess to deliver us, His children, from destruction and to our destiny!

DISCUSSION QUESTIONS

1. Can you detect any evidence that you are entangled in your own culture?

2. How do you plan to fight that entanglement?

3. Is there anything in your life that has the focus of your attention more than God?

4. If you suspect that your answer to the previous question is yes, what impact might that gaze have upon your children?

5. What kind of legacy do you want to leave for your children? How are you making that happen today?

CHAPTER 6

One Wife Too Many
(The Young and the Restless)

We've been detouring in the land of Sodom and Gomorrah for a few chapters in order to study Lot and his family. Now let's return to our exploration of Abraham and his immediate family line. We want to see how God worked beneath, behind, through, above, and beyond his family mess.

Even though there was a great deal of family mess going on in Abraham's immediate family, I want you to notice something: God did not hesitate to proclaim Himself the God of Abraham, Isaac, and Jacob. God did not run from the family mess of this family. On the contrary, He identified Himself as the God of this family. Isn't that encouraging for you in your family mess, too? He's not going to run from you just because you've got a mess on your hands.

Now we come to the third major mess of Abraham's family mess.

● The first mess had to do with Abraham leaving Babylonia

and his father's house.

- The second mess had to do with God separating Lot from Abraham.

- The third mess has to do with Abraham's wife.

Let's look at Genesis sixteen:

> Now Sarai, Abram's wife had borne him no children, and she had an Egyptian maid whose name was Hagar. So Sarai said to Abram, "Now behold, the LORD has prevented me from bearing children. Please go in to my maid; perhaps I will obtain children through her." And Abram listened to the voice of Sarai.
>
> After Abram had lived ten years in the land of Canaan, Abram's wife Sarai took Hagar the Egyptian, her maid, and gave her to her husband Abram as his wife. He went in to Hagar, and she conceived; and when she saw that she had conceived, her mistress was despised in her sight.
>
> And Sarai said to Abram, "May the wrong done me be upon you. I gave my maid into your arms, but when she saw that she had conceived, I was despised in her sight. May the LORD judge between you and me."

But Abram said to Sarai, "Behold, your maid is in your power; do to her what is good in your sight." So Sarai treated her harshly, and she fled from her presence.

Now the angel of the LORD found her by a spring of water in the wilderness, by the spring on the way to Shur. He said, "Hagar, Sarai's maid, where have you come from and where are you going?" And she said, "I am fleeing from the presence of my mistress Sarai." Then the angel of the LORD said to her, "Return to your mistress, and submit yourself to her authority." Moreover, the angel of the LORD said to her, "I will greatly multiply your descendants so that they will be too many to count."

The angel of the LORD said to her further, "Behold, you are with child, And you will bear a son; And you shall call his name Ishmael, Because the LORD has given heed to your affliction. He will be a wild donkey of a man, His hand will be against everyone, And everyone's hand will be against him; And he will live to the east of all his brothers."

Then she called the name of the LORD who spoke to her, "You are a God who sees"; for she said, "Have I even remained alive here after seeing Him?" Therefore the well was called Beer-lahai-roi; behold, it is between Kadesh and Bered (Genesis 16:1–14).

Here Sarah is still called Sarai and Abraham is still called Abram, but for convenience, we will call them Sarah and Abraham.

The lack of children, particularly a male heir, was one of the most formidable problems of Abraham's life. God had given Abraham a tremendous promise of making a great nation out of him, and doing that through a son who would be his heir. God had even told Abraham that his descendents would be as numerous as the stars of Heaven and the grains of sand on the seashores of the world, which, by the way, are roughly equivalent of 10^{18}. That's a lot. And yet Abraham had trouble believing these promises of God because he and his wife were old and past the childbearing years. This is where we pick up the story.

Sarah had borne Abraham no children. To Sarah, this was the curse of God. She believed that God had prevented her from having children. To understand this passage of Scripture, you will need to understand a little bit about the culture and prevailing norms of that time.

Women during that time believed that children were a gift from the Lord. The more children they had, the more favor they believed they had in God's eyes. They also believed, conversely, that if they had no children God had cursed them. So children were of prime importance to women of that time. This is hard to understand today, isn't it, since so many believe that children are a curse and that the fewer you have the more blessed you are!

Armed with this understanding, we are able to relate to Sarah.

She had to do something about her childlessness. Sarah was one of "The Young and the Restless." She could not trust in or wait upon the promise of God. It doesn't seem to dawn on her to pray, so instead she offers Abraham her personal servant as a concubine or surrogate wife and mother.

Before you judge Sarah too harshly, understand that this was probably the custom of people of the day. But the question isn't, was this the custom of the world? but was it the plan of God? Your answer should be *no!* How do I know? Because I have read through the Bible more than twenty times. I know what God's will and plan for marriage entails, and His will and plan is one man for one woman for a lifetime.

Genesis 2:24 says, *"For this reason a man shall leave his father and his mother, and be joined to his wife; and they shall become one flesh."* And Mark 10:9 tops it off: *"What therefore God has joined together, let no man separate."*

In the case of Adam and Eve, they were the only two people on earth. In time they would have children, but these children were ineligible for marriage. So it seems to be clear from God's Word and the circumstances that it was His will for Adam and Eve to have one mate for their lifetime.

We have something that Adam and Eve didn't have: a completed canon or set of books of the Word of God. When you read the complete canon of the Word of God, you will see that God did allow remarriage in the case of death. Preachers and scholars disagree over the various conditions of remarriage, but let us agree that at a minimum God intended one man for one woman at a time. So Sarah's offer was not in keeping with God's will and plan.

We also know that it was not God's will for Abraham to have a child through his wife's handmaid, because God had given him a promise about his own children through Sarah. Nevertheless, Abraham listened to the voice of his wife instead of the voice of God.

Once again we see Abraham's difficulty in trusting Jehovah God. Once again we see Abraham's difficulty in assertively confronting one of his relatives. And once again we see that it leads to family mess. He could not confront Lot about leaving Babylon with him and he did not confront his wife about her offer. We have no way of knowing, but it seems reasonable to assume that this offer also appealed to Abraham's flesh. Be that as it may, family mess began when Abraham listened to his wife instead of trusting in the promise of God.

This was Adam's problem, too. If we go back to the Garden, we find out that this was what God listed as the major reason why Adam was about to experience the consequences of sin.

> Then to Adam He said, "Because you have listened to the voice of your wife, and have eaten from the tree about which I commanded you, saying, 'You shall not eat from it'; cursed is the ground because of you; in toil you will eat of it all the days of your life. Both thorns and thistles it shall grow for you;

and you will eat the plants of the field; by the sweat of your face you will eat bread, till you return to the ground, because from it you were taken; for you are dust, and to dust you shall return" (Genesis 3:17–19).

Family mess entered the world when Adam listened to his wife instead of trusting in God. And that same family mess is playing itself out in the narrative before us.

If you're a husband, there will come a time when your wife will offer you an alternative plan to the command and will of God. Family mess! Your response to that offer will determine the intensity of the family mess that you will experience and pass on to your posterity.

You must obey God rather than man. You must obey God's Word rather than your wife. You must do all that you can to please your wife, but God's Word has to come first.

So Abraham went into Sarah's handmaid, Hagar, and she conceived. This was certainly a fall, like Adam's, and the author seems to be relating it to the first fall.

Husband, when that time comes that your wife fights against you and offers you an alternative to the will of God, if you follow her not only will you encounter family mess, but she will have little respect for you. There is the problem: You have to treat her with love, but you have to stand your ground. Now, that's a hard thing to do. Most of us men can treat our wives with love but we can't hold our ground. Some of us can hold our ground but we can't treat our wives with love. We have to do both.

When Abraham went into Hagar, he started something that plagued the children of Israel for thousands of years: polygamy—the practice of having more than one wife. The cultures around Abraham practiced polygamy freely, but this is the first reference to it among God's chosen people. The family mess that Abraham planted that day would bear fruit and one day be a part of the cause of the nation of Israel going into captivity.

Hundreds of years later we come to Solomon with his three hundred wives and seven hundred concubines. A thousand women! These were not just regular marriages, but political alliances with the nations of the earth. The Bible tells us that these foreign women turned his heart away from God. God then allowed the kingdom to break up and, ultimately, the Israelites to go into captivity. Just remember how that got started: Abraham and Sarah and Hagar.

When Hagar saw that she was pregnant, she despised her mistress. She now had something Sarah didn't have. She also shared something with Abraham that he and Sarah didn't share. It appeared that Hagar had God's blessing and that Sarah was cursed.

The family mess increased when Abraham had to deal with two wives instead of one, *and* a child on the way. Abraham had one wife too many. It has been said that a man is too much man for one woman but not enough man for two women, so you're going to have to settle for one. If Abraham had trouble dealing with one wife, he would have double trouble dealing with two.

Perhaps the main potential for devastating family mess was Abraham's temptation to use Ishmael as his heir instead of waiting upon God's promise. Satan wanted Abraham to settle for second best instead of the divine blessing that God wanted to bestow. Satan wants all men of God to settle for second best rather than experience the divine blessing, promise, and destiny that God has in store for us. Husband, Satan might try to use your wife to trick you out of receiving the promise of God. Be on guard.

Abraham had constant turmoil in his home because of these two wives. Sarah's plan to ingratiate herself to her husband backfired, and when she saw that Hagar despised her, she complained to Abraham.

So, what did Abraham do? He did what he normally did—nothing. He did not confront his wife or protect the rights of his second wife and coming child. Instead, he allowed Sarah to do whatever she wanted to do. Abraham, in my opinion, was a passive man who had trouble trusting God. But God was making him into a man of courage and faith in spite of his family mess.

When you read in the New Testament that Abraham is called the father of faith, you ought not to attribute that to the natural ability of Abraham. You ought to attribute it to God working supremely and sovereignly in the life of a man, and in spite of the family mess that you see, to make him into something that would last throughout eternity. It ought to make you praise God when you realize there was no way in the world that Abraham, on his own, could become the father of faith. He was weak in his flesh and he had family mess, but still God made him into something great. That ought to give you hope.

When Sarah saw Hagar's attitude, she treated Hagar harshly. Hagar had to run from her presence. The two women couldn't live in the same tent, and the same is true today.

Now the angel of the Lord found Hagar and spoke to her. I believe this is another pre-incarnate appearance of Christ. The first thing He told her to do was go back to Sarah and submit to her authority. Now there is a strange bit of advice. Not many modern Christians want to understand it, much less live it out. But God's answer to the situation was to go back and go through the pain because He had something He wanted to do for Hagar in the midst of her family mess.

No, God did not tell her to find her own apartment, file for legal separation, or sue for a divorce. He told her to be an adult. Adulthood is the ability to face the reality of your situation and have the courage to make the best of it through the power of the Holy Spirit. Sometimes God works in the midst of family mess.

I'm not suggesting that anyone stay in an abusive situation. I am merely pointing out that we all have some messy situations that we want to run from. Some of them we should run from, but we ought to seek God to find out which ones are which. There are some messy situations that God wants to deliver us from, and there are some messy situations that God wants to take us through.

God went on to tell Hagar what He was going to do for her, right in Abraham's house, right before her enemy, Sarah. This reminds me of the words of David in Psalm 23: *"Thou preparest a table before me in the presence of mine enemies: thou anointest my head with oil; my cup runneth over"* (Psalm 23:5, KJV). When God wants to give you a promise and a blessing, no enemy or family mess can thwart Him.

He promised Hagar two things:

- *I will greatly multiply your descendents so that they will be too many to count.* Now she would really be considered blessed, and not by her own hands.

- *I will give you a son.* Children were considered a blessing of God, but a son was a special blessing because the family line was carried on through the son.

Our first response to affliction is to try to get out of it. But sometimes our family mess is a conduit through which God wants to give us a promise and a blessing. *God doesn't always move the mountain; sometimes He gives us the strength to climb it.*

We mentioned before that God sometimes separates us from

family mess. Yes, He does! But I have to tell you that sometimes He sends you back into it. And not just back into it, but back to submit to someone's authority. That's not so much fun, is it? But sometimes it's God's way.

Here we see that Abraham's family mess was going to result in even more family mess. God told Hagar that Ishmael was going to be a wild donkey of a man who would be against everyone and whom everyone would be against. He was going to live to the east of the Israelites. As we have seen, living and traveling east seemed to imply going the way of the world as opposed to the way of God. Hagar was going to give birth to another nation of enemies against Israel. The people to whom Joseph was sold by his brothers are called Ishmaelites in Genesis 37:25. This group of people became the Arab nations, still Israel's enemies today.

Even though His blessing will result in more enemies against His chosen people, God has compassion on Hagar and blesses her. So Hagar calls God "the God who sees me" (Genesis 16:13b, NIV). She even recognized the compassion of God in allowing her to see Him and yet live. Our God is a God who sees us!

He sees us in our most desperate hour. He has His all-seeing eye on us. We are the apple of His eye. We are the pupil, the most tender portion, of His eye. He is watching over us. He knows just how much we can bear.

Paul spoke to this:

No temptation has overtaken you but such as is

common to man; and God is faithful, who will not allow you to be tempted beyond what you are able, but with the temptation will provide the way of escape also, so that you will be able to endure it (1 Corinthians 10:13).

As the curtain drops on this narrative, we get information on Abraham's age. Why? Because it helps us to understand the impact of family mess. He was 86 when Ishmael was born. In chapter 21 we find out that he was 100 when Isaac was born. It may be that Sarah's idea to bear a child through Hagar actually delayed the promise of God for fourteen years.

Nevertheless, God, being the compassionate God that He is, eventually blessed Sarah with a son—one who would be in the line of the coming Messiah. God is the God of Abraham, Abraham's son (Isaac), and Abraham's grandson (Jacob). Can you believe that God knows how to work beneath, behind, through, above, and beyond family mess?

There are several big lessons that we should learn here:

- *God's promises and plans cannot be stopped by family mess.* What God wants to do in your life cannot be stopped by family mess. It can be stopped by your sin, but not by family mess.

- *God's promises and plans can be delayed by family mess.* Sometimes what God wants to do He delays because of the mess that's going on.

- *Family mess is very messy and painful.*

- *Family mess breeds more family mess.*

- *If we want to hasten our rise above family sin and family mess, we must not be "Young and Restless."* We must be mature, trusting, and patient. When God is ready, it will come. It is no use creating family mess to try to hurry God up, because we'll only slow down the promises.

- *If we want to hasten our rise above family sin and family mess, we must accept God's vision for our posterity.* Sarah was unwilling to accept God's vision. She had her own plan. "You aren't moving, Lord, and I don't know what You're going to do and I don't have any children, so I'm going to give Hagar to Abraham." She took matters into her own hands and look what happened! We have to learn to accept God's vision for our posterity. We have to not only accept it but also trust it.

DISCUSSION QUESTIONS

1. Are there any situations in your life in which someone is offering you a shortcut to the plan of God?

2. Are you a get-it-done-myself kind of person or a wait-for the-will-of-God kind of person? Justify your answer.

3. On a scale of 1 to 10, with 1 being the lowest and 10 being the highest, rate your maturity, your trust in God, and your patience with God's plan. Please explain each rating.

4. In what ways might family mess delay your possession of God's blessing and destiny in your life?

5. In what ways is God making you aware of His destiny for you in spite of family mess?

CHAPTER 7

In the Image of Your Father
(One Life to Live)

We've looked at how Sarah and Abraham tried to hurry God up by bearing a son through Hagar. And we've seen how that backfired, as family mess so often does. Now let's make a jump. In this chapter I want to talk about Isaac— the heir of promise. But because I want to talk about him as an adult, I thought I'd better give you an overview of what happened between these two stories.

Genesis 21 through 24 tell about how God was faithful to His promise and gave Abraham and Sarah a child of their own. These chapters tell the story of Isaac's birth, circumcision, childhood, and the strain caused by the presence of Ishmael, Hagar's son. They tell how God tested Abraham's faith by asking him to sacrifice Isaac—and then preventing him from going through with it. And they tell of Sarah's death. Finally, these chapters recount the story of how Rebekah became Isaac's wife.

Isaac is the second generation after Abraham. We're now ready to look at the impact of family mess in his life and God's providence in spite of the family mess. Let's begin by reading a passage from Genesis twenty-six:

> Now there was a famine in the land, besides the previous famine that had occurred in the days of Abraham. So Isaac went to Gerar, to Abimelech king of the Philistines.
>
> The LORD appeared to him and said, "Do not go down to Egypt; stay in the land of which I shall tell you. Sojourn in this land and I will be with you and bless you, for to you and to your descendants I will give all these lands, and I will establish the oath which I swore to your father Abraham. I will multiply your descendants as the stars of heaven, and will give your descendants all these lands; and by your descendants all the nations of the earth shall be blessed; because Abraham obeyed Me and kept My charge, My commandments, My statutes and My laws" (Genesis 26:1–5).

We come now to an important experience in the life of Isaac, the biological son of Abraham and the heir that God had promised to Abraham and Sarah. It came about that there was a famine in the land. In order to survive, Isaac went to the Philistine city of Gerar, where Abimelech the king of the Philistines lived. While Isaac was at Gerar, God appeared to him, gave him some instructions, and extended to him the promise He'd given his father, Abraham. God told Isaac not to go down to Egypt but to sojourn in the land of the Philistines.

He also said He would do four things for him: *"I will be with you; I will bless you; I will give all of these lands to you and your descendants; and I will establish the oath I swore to your father Abraham."* Let's look at these four in order:

First, God promised that *He would always be with Isaac.* What more could Isaac want than the company of God? What more could *we* want than the company of God? In fact, we have more than Isaac did. The Bible says that all three persons of the Trinity—God, Jesus Christ, and the Holy Spirit—dwell within us.

In Matthew 28, Jesus gave the Great Commission:

> "Go therefore and make disciples of all the nations, baptizing them in the name of the Father and the Son and the Holy Spirit, teaching them to observe all that I commanded you; and lo, I am with you always, even to the end of the age" (Matthew 28:19–20).

In the Greek, the phrase *I am with you always* literally means "I am with you all days." Jesus is telling us He will be with us during all kinds of days. He will be with us during dark days, difficult days, depressing days, discouraging days, distracted days, and despairing days. God has promised to be with us all our days. What a promise!

The second thing God promised Isaac was that *He would bless him*. Who else could bless Isaac but Jehovah God, the Source of all blessing? Likewise, who else can bless us but God?

God has already blessed us. Paul said in Ephesians, *"Blessed be the God and Father of our Lord Jesus Christ, who has blessed us with every spiritual blessing in the heavenly places in Christ"* (Ephesians 1:3).

Here is a partial list of the spiritual blessings with which God has blessed us:

- election,
- predestination,
- regeneration,
- redemption,
- justification,
- divine providence, and
- glorification.

The third promise to Isaac was God's reaffirmation of His oath to give Abraham's descendents the Promised Land: *"I will give all of these lands to you and your descendants."*

For Christians, the Promised Land is abundant Christian living. And eventually, we'll enter the New Jerusalem. God doesn't just want to save us; He wants to give us the abundant Christian life, too. Jesus said, *"The thief comes only to steal and kill and destroy; I came that they may have life, and have it abundantly"*

(John 10:10). God promises us all these blessings.

With this fourth promise, God extends to Isaac the promises that He had made to Abraham. The Lord then recounts the particulars of that oath:

- I will multiply your descendants as the stars of Heaven.
- I will give your descendants all these lands.
- By your descendants all the nations of the earth shall be blessed. *Jesus*

Among Isaac's descendants would be the greatest kings of Israel, including David and Solomon. Isaac's descendants also included Jesus Christ. Jesus received His legal right to the throne of David from his adoptive father, Joseph, who was in the line of Isaac. Scholars believe that Mary was also in the line of David, so Jesus got a double dose. And all of the nations of the earth for all time would be blessed in Jesus Christ.

After listing the promises, God told Isaac the reason they were still good and being extended to him: *"because Abraham obeyed Me and kept My charge, My commandments, My statutes and My laws"* (Genesis 26:5).

What powerful proof that God can work through family mess to bring a man to his destiny. Abraham, the man we have seen struggle with trust in and obedience to God, received from God's own mouth the testimony that he had kept God's commandments, statutes, and laws.

We can now take up the other side of the verses upon which this book is based. Let us return to Exodus 20.

> "You shall not worship them or serve them; for I, the LORD your God, am a jealous God, visiting the iniquity of the fathers on the children, on the third and the fourth generations of those who hate Me, *but showing lovingkindness to thousands, to those who love Me and keep My commandments"* (Exodus 20:5–6, emphasis mine).

As I explained in an earlier chapter, the idea of retribution includes punishment for sin and reward for righteousness. It works both ways. God will visit on His people both the consequences for the iniquity of their fathers *and* the lovingkindness demonstrated by fathers who loved God and kept His commandments. It was because of Abraham's love for God and obedience that God was showing His lovingkindness to Isaac.

We talk about all the bad things that happen to us because of what our mother or father did wrong. "I'm messed up because my mother never read to me" or "I'm this way because my father never told me he loved me." We feel cursed because of what happened to us in the past. But is it also possible that you are *blessed* on account of what happened in the past?

I am experiencing the consequences of the sins of my forefathers. But I am also experiencing the lovingkindness of God because of my forefathers' love for God and obedience to

His commandments. My father is a preacher and my grandfather was a preacher and there are religious people on both sides of my family. Therefore, it is possible and probable that some of the lovingkindness of God that I am experiencing is a result of my forefathers' godliness.

Let me give you another important thought: It is possible that the lovingkindness of God that my children are experiencing is a result of *my* love and obedience to God, as well as that of my forefathers.

The lovingkindness God showed to Abraham lasted all the way to the birth of Jesus Christ and beyond. Over in Matthew where Mary is overshadowed by the power of the Holy Spirit and a child was placed within her, she told Elizabeth that this was the promise to Abraham. To Abraham! More than four generations away, wouldn't you say? Try forty-two generations. The promise to Abraham ran through Abraham, Isaac, Jacob, Joseph, and all the way down to Jesus Christ.

Love God and obey His commandments for your children's sake, and for your grandchildren and great-grandchildren's sake. Who knows how far down the line that blessing will be visited? Blessings will come to them because of your faithfulness. How about that for another good reason to love and obey God?

Let's take a look now at the rest of the story.

> So Isaac lived in Gerar. When the men of the place asked about his wife, he said, "She is my sister," for

he was afraid to say, "my wife," thinking, "the men of the place might kill me on account of Rebekah, for she is beautiful."

It came about, when he had been there a long time, that Abimelech king of the Philistines looked out through a window, and saw, and behold, Isaac was caressing his wife Rebekah.

Then Abimelech called Isaac and said, "Behold, certainly she is your wife! How then did you say, 'She is my sister'?" And Isaac said to him, "Because I said, 'I might die on account of her.'"

Abimelech said, "What is this you have done to us? One of the people might easily have lain with your wife, and you would have brought guilt upon us."

So Abimelech charged all the people, saying, "He who touches this man or his wife shall surely be put to death."

Now Isaac sowed in that land and reaped in the same year a hundredfold. And the LORD blessed him (Genesis 26:6–12).

It is obvious that Isaac did not trust God to deliver him from Gerar and his countrymen. He felt he had to take matters into his own hands and come up with a deception. But despite Isaac's lack of trust, God delivered him anyway—probably because he was the son of Abraham.

More often than we are aware of it, we and our children experience deliverance from evil because of the righteousness of our forefathers.

Now if this were all there was to the story, it would be interesting enough. But there is something that is perhaps more important than this for those of us who are Bible readers. Isaac had only "One Life to Live" and he seems to have lived it almost identically to his father. This incident in the life of Isaac is almost identical to an incident in the life of his father, Abraham. Let's look at Genesis 20:1-5:

> Now Abraham journeyed from there toward the land of the Negev, and settled between Kadesh and Shur; then he sojourned in Gerar. Abraham said of Sarah his wife, "She is my sister." So Abimelech king of Gerar sent and took Sarah.

> But God came to Abimelech in a dream of the night, and said to him, "Behold, you are a dead man because of the woman whom you have taken, for she is married." Now Abimelech had not come near her; and he said, "Lord, will You slay a nation, even though blameless? Did he not himself say to me, 'She is my sister'? And she herself said, 'He is my brother.' In the integrity of my heart and the innocence of my hands I have done this" (Genesis 20:1–18).

The two stories are so close it's remarkable. Notice:

- Abraham sojourned in Gerar, and his son sojourned in Gerar.

- Abimelech was the king in Gerar when Abraham sojourned there. Abimelech, either the same king or a descendant, was the king in Gerar when Isaac sojourned there.

- Evidently there was inquiry about Abraham's wife as there was about Isaac's wife.

- Abraham lied about Sarah, saying, "She is my sister." Isaac lied about Rebekah, saying, "She is my sister."

- God providentially intervened in both situations and no serious complications occurred.

This is amazing! How could two people, even a father and son, have such similar incidents? How could Isaac's actions so closely resemble those of his father? Why did God choose to record these two incidents in the pages of holy writ?

I'm not sure I have all the answers to these questions, but I would like to take a stab at them based upon forty-nine years of life, forty-one years of Christianity, twenty-seven years of pastoral ministry, and reading through various translations of the Bible more than twenty times.

First, the consequences of the sins of the father are visited upon the children to the third and fourth generations. It is possible that Abraham related the story of his experiences with Abimelech to Isaac, and Isaac consciously or subconsciously emulated the actions of his father. But it is also possible that Abraham did not. Either way, we can be reasonably sure that Isaac struggled in some of the same ways as his father:

- He loved beautiful women.
- He had trouble trusting God in difficult situations.
- He would lie if he felt his life was in danger.

We see before us more than just the consequences of Abraham's sins being passed on to Isaac: *We see the very image of his father being passed on to him.* There is a Scripture that I think applies here. *"When Adam had lived one hundred and thirty years, he became the father of a son in his own likeness, according to his image, and named him Seth"* (Genesis 5:3).

Now that is indeed interesting, since the Bible says something very similar when Adam was created: *"Then God said, 'Let Us make man in Our image, according to Our likeness; and let them rule over the fish of the sea and over the birds of the sky and over the cattle and over all the earth, and over every creeping thing that creeps on the earth'"* (Genesis 1:26).

- Adam was made in God's image and likeness; everyone born after Adam is born in Adam's image and likeness.

- Adam was created innocent and sinless; everyone born

after Adam is born in sin and shaped in iniquity.

- Adam was created with God's moral image and likeness; everyone born after Adam is a fallen image-bearer who is radically corrupted by sin.

Because of the sin of Adam we not only receive the punishment and the consequences of the sins of our fathers and forefathers all the way back to Adam, but we also receive the unique sin nature of our parents and their family lines.

Locked in the infinitely complex genetic code of our parents are the unique qualities, characteristics, idiosyncrasies, and sins of our family lines, and we receive all of this from our parents. We have but "One Life to Live." Without the divine intervention of God, Jesus Christ, the Holy Spirit, salvation, and His providence, we will live it out more like our parents than we would ever imagine. In other words, *the probability for reenacting the family mess of our own families is very high.*

Thank God for His divine intervention and providence in the lives of His people. Providence is God's faithful care and effective guidance of everything He has made toward the ends He has chosen. He chose Abraham, called Abraham, sanctified Abraham, and guided Abraham to the positive destiny He had planned for him.

Even in the midst of Abraham's struggle to trust God, his passivity, and his lying, did you notice that God called him a prophet? Did you notice that He blessed the prayers of Abraham to bring about the healing and deliverance of Abimelech's household?

Thank God for His divine intervention and providence, not only in the life of Abraham, but in the life of his son, Isaac. He blessed Isaac and extended to him the promise of his father because of the love and obedience of Abraham. God blessed Isaac and was not ashamed to be called the God of Abraham and Isaac. That was Isaac's destiny. And that destiny was based upon the grace of God.

There is not much in the Bible about Isaac's accomplishments. He was the digger of wells—but his enemies filled up most of his wells. It seems that Isaac did not accomplish a great deal. But he was blessed because of his father's love and obedience toward God.

Thank God for His divine intervention and providence in *our* lives. Through the miracle of salvation, Jesus Christ was the Lamb that was slain before the foundation of the world. God chose us in Christ before the foundation of the world. He chose us and called us that we might bring glory to His name: *"These whom He predestined, He also called; and these whom He called, He also justified; and these whom He justified, He also glorified"* (Romans 8:30).

He called us with a holy calling—out of darkness into His marvelous light—to be His children: children of freedom, hope, and destiny.

In short, God has called us to rise above family mess, and He will give us an inheritance among those who are righteous. Since we each have only "One Life to Live," we should leave a godly inheritance to our children, our children's children, and as many as the Lord our God shall call.

DISCUSSION QUESTIONS

1. What level of awareness do you have regarding any family sins?

2. Are any of these family sins impacting you personally? If so, in what ways? If not, what makes you think you escaped from their impact?

3. In what ways has God intervened in your life to help you rise above the legacy of your family sin and family mess?

CHAPTER 8

Jacob and Esau
(The Young and the Restless)

We've looked at two generations of Abraham's family: Abraham and Isaac. Now let's look at the third, because, remember, God will repay to the third and fourth generation—the sins and the faithfulness—of what the fathers have done. So let's look at Isaac's son, Jacob.

Isaac's wife, Rebekah, was barren. So Isaac prayed for her and she became pregnant. That is interesting in and of itself, isn't it? When we can't have children, what do we do? We go to specialists. But what did they do? They prayed. What an idea!

But instead of one baby on the way there were two, and the babies struggled within her. This was so disturbing to Rebekah that she asked herself the question, "If I am pregnant, what is going on inside of me?" So, she went to inquire of the Lord.

The LORD said to her, *"Two nations are in your womb; and two peoples will be separated from your body; and one people shall be stronger than the other; and the older shall serve the younger"* (Genesis 25:23).

This third generation of Abraham's family begins with family mess in the womb. This is a remarkable Scripture! Maybe you're asking, "How can twins struggle even before birth?" The only explanation I can give you is the genetics of their mother and father. This was an indication of what was to come.

When it came time for Rebekah to deliver the babies, Esau came out first. They named him Esau, which means *hairy,* because he was covered with red hair. Esau's brother came out after him. He was holding onto Esau's heel, so they named him Jacob, which means "one who grasps the heel" or "one who supplants or cheats." Family mess marked the gestation of Jacob and Esau and family mess attended their birth. But the worst was yet to come.

As Jacob and Esau grew up, you could readily see the family mess. One of the problems was parental partiality. Parental partiality fostered continuing hostility between Esau, the opportunistic outdoorsman and hunter, beloved of his father; and Jacob, the quiet, settled, introverted—but sneaky—person, favored by his mother.

The tensions between these brothers seemed to threaten the fulfillment of the divine promise to make a great nation through Abraham, Isaac, and his heir. But which one of the twins would be that heir?

Esau was the firstborn, and as such owned the birthright. This birthright was a double portion of the father's assets upon his death. Part of the firstborn's benefits also were a special blessing from the father and the privilege of leadership of the family. The Bible says that Esau despised this birthright (Genesis 25:34), but Jacob coveted it.

It is doubtful that either of the boys understood the long-term importance of the birthright. They certainly didn't understand that it would lead genealogically to the birth of the promised Messiah. Neither did Jacob understand that he coveted something from his earthly father that was already bequeathed to him from his heavenly Father. Notice these verses:

> When Jacob had cooked stew, Esau came in from the field and he was famished; and Esau said to Jacob, "Please let me have a swallow of that red stuff there, for I am famished." Therefore his name was called Edom.
>
> But Jacob said, "First sell me your birthright."
>
> Esau said, "Behold, I am about to die; so of what use then is the birthright to me?"
>
> And Jacob said, "First swear to me"; so he swore to him, and sold his birthright to Jacob. Then Jacob gave Esau bread and lentil stew; and he ate and drank, and rose and went on his way. Thus Esau despised his birthright (Genesis 25:29–34).

Evidently Esau wasn't starving or about to die, or the Bible wouldn't have made that last comment about him despising his birthright. He was just hungry. He thought so little of his birthright and his heritage that he sold it for a can of Campbell's vegetable soup.

The first lesson we can learn from this particular family mess is this: The birthright of your father is important, but your earthly father cannot give you what can only be obtained from your heavenly Father. Therefore, do not ingratiate yourself with your earthly father just to get better stuff in the inheritance, but receive and rest on the birthright that has been promised to you by your heavenly Father.

When you accepted Jesus Christ as your Lord and Savior, you were born into the family of God and adopted into the royal family. Believe it and rest in it. This will allow you to rise above the family mess that may come about when everyone else is caught up in achieving, obtaining, or stealing your earthly father's inheritance.

Which of us has not experienced parental or family partiality in some way? Everyone has. Well, I've got good news for you: *The birthright of Heaven is more important than the birthright of earth.* We have received the authority to be sons and daughters of God. From the birthright of earth we receive an earthly inheritance, but from the birthright of heaven we receive a heavenly inheritance.

We are heirs of the promises of God and joint-heirs with Jesus

Christ. We have received eternal life.

We have received a destiny that includes an inheritance among those who are righteous.

We don't have to struggle for something that God has already given us. Yet all around me I see people struggling in their families trying to get something out of them: trying to get something from their mother, trying to get something from their father, trying to get something from their brothers and sisters—something that can only come through Jesus Christ.

As we continue to explore the history of Jacob and Esau, it should be coming clear that we are looking at the history of "The Young and the Restless." We see Esau's youth and restlessness at the end of the twenty-sixth chapter of Genesis. Here the author tells us that Esau married two heathen women and brought grief to Isaac and Rebekah. Anyone who has parented a child can understand the grief that Isaac and Rebekah must've felt.

But Jacob was young and restless, too.

> Now it came about, when Isaac was old and his eyes were too dim to see, that he called his older son Esau and said to him, "My son." And he said to him, "Here I am."
>
> Isaac said, "Behold now, I am old and I do not know the day of my death. Now then, please take

> your gear, your quiver and your bow, and go out
> to the field and hunt game for me; and prepare a
> savory dish for me such as I love, and bring it to
> me that I may eat, so that my soul may bless you
> before I die" (Genesis 27:1–4).

In the Jewish economy, the father would bestow upon the oldest son "the blessing." This was God's covenant blessing that was passed to one's offspring. The blessing entailed personal, relational, prophetic, and spiritual aspects.

So Esau went hunting. But Rebekah had overheard the conversation. She went to her favorite son, Jacob, and told him what was about to happen, and then she told him to follow her plan to steal the blessing. Notice these verses:

> Rebekah said to her son Jacob, "Behold, I heard
> your father speak to your brother Esau, saying,
> 'Bring me some game and prepare a savory dish
> for me, that I may eat, and bless you in the
> presence of the LORD before my death.'
>
> "Now therefore, my son, listen to me as I command
> you. Go now to the flock and bring me two choice
> young goats from there, that I may prepare them
> as a savory dish for your father, such as he loves.
> Then you shall bring it to your father, that he may
> eat, so that he may bless you before his death"
> (Genesis 27:6–10).

Evidently, Rebekah coveted the blessing for her son as much as he coveted it for himself. But Jacob saw a flaw in her plan. *"My brother is a hairy man and I am a smooth man,"* he said. *"If my father feels me, I will get a curse instead of a blessing."*

But Rebekah said, *"Let the curse be on me. You just do what I tell you to do!"*

So Jacob obeyed the voice of his mother instead of relying upon the promise of God. Sound familiar? It's just what Isaac did when he obeyed the voice of Rebekah, what Abraham did when he obeyed the voice of Sarah, and what Adam did when he obeyed the voice of Eve.

Dear brother, if you would be a man of God you must cultivate the ability to trust in the Word and promises of God in the face of pressure from important women in your life.

Back at the ranch, Rebekah made the dish Isaac liked and put the skin of the young goats on Jacob's hands and on the back of his neck to make him feel like Esau. Then Jacob went in to his father and tricked him out of the blessing. Family mess!

Jacob was a supplanter, a cheater, and a trickster—and his mother was, too. We have seen how the sins or consequences of the father are passed on to the children to the third and fourth generations. But now we see that it works with mothers, too. Jacob was not only being impacted by his father's family mess, but his mother's family mess as well. We are going to see in another chapter that Rebekah got her deceptive nature from her own family line.

What a sad situation. Isaac loved Esau, and Jacob obviously coveted that love. Rebekah loved Jacob, and we're not sure what kind of impact that had upon Esau, but it was probably negative. Here is a father and a mother tearing their own family apart. This led to more family mess.

If you, dear brother or sister, have children, then I would ask you to consider whether you might have shown partiality for one over the other. I'm not holding you responsible for all your children's actions; I'm simply asking you to consider whether or not you might have contributed anything to the problem by favoring one over the other. If so, do everything you can to make it right.

Esau sold Jacob the birthright and Jacob tricked Esau out of the blessing—but none of it had to happen. Jacob's birthright and blessing had already been prophesied and fixed. Jacob coveted things from his earthly father that were already his from his Heavenly Father. He wrestled with his earthly father for that which was already his from his Heavenly Father. Please notice these thoughts:

- Jacob didn't realize who he was—the progenitor of Jesus Christ.

- Jacob didn't realize the magnificent promises that were his.

• Jacob didn't realize his destiny.

It's a sad fact of life that we often struggle to get from our families that which we already have in Jesus Christ. "I just wish my mother would show love to me." Well, I've got somebody better than that who can love you, and His name is Jesus. "I just wish that somebody would approve of something I do." I've got somebody who can give you eternal approval, and His name is Jesus.

Our heavenly heritage is in Jesus Christ—our identity ought also to be in Jesus Christ. We are priests and kings who have been born into the family of God and adopted into His royal family. We have magnificent promises in our Lord and Savior, Jesus Christ. Our destiny is to reign with Jesus Christ from the throne of David in the New Jerusalem. We ought to rest in that inheritance and stop struggling so hard for earthly inheritance.

Back to the story. As soon as Jacob went out from his father, having stolen the blessing, Esau came in from the field with his dish of savory meat. Isaac asked, "Who are you?" and Jacob said, "I am your firstborn son, Esau!"

Now we come to the height of family mess. The Bible says that Isaac trembled violently because he realized that he had been tricked. He told his son what had happened. Esau cried a great and bitter cry and begged for a blessing—but alas, that which he once took for granted was now gone. So Esau swore to kill his brother.

Rebekah called Jacob and told him about his brother's threats. Then she told him to go to live with her brother, Laban, until Esau's anger subsided. Her sin separated her from the son she loved and sent him like a vagrant through the land. Though the Bible doesn't say one way or another, it appears that Rebekah never saw Jacob again.

Let's survey the family mess:

- *Isaac trembled at the deception.* It appears that Isaac was devastated. We don't know what happened with his relationship with Rebekah, because there are no more references to her in the Old Testament except when she is buried, but we have to imagine that this incident probably damaged their relationship beyond repair.

- *Esau was tormented, angered, embittered, and vengeful.*

- *Rebekah was, no doubt, greatly grieved by the departure of her beloved son who in all probability she never saw again.*

- *Jacob was bereft of his whole family, his home, his homeland, and his peace.* He traveled to the homeland and people of his mother—only to be cheated and tricked himself.

Let me offer some observations to wrap up this portion of our study of the history of Abraham's family:

1. It is now clear that the consequences of the sins of Abraham were passed on to Isaac and that the consequences of both their sins were passed on to Jacob. Someone needed to stop this deadly chain through repentance.

Praise God that we can stop some of the mess in our families—if we repent. We can't stop all of it, but we can make life significantly different for our children. If we don't repent, our children will have to carry and finish our pain. Are you willing to say, "The buck stops here—I will be the last link in the chain of this family mess"? I pray you will be that last link.

2. The patterns of dysfunctional families (don't talk; don't feel; don't trust) are evident in the lives of Abraham, his son, and his grandson.

Abraham didn't talk much; he was very passive. Isaac didn't talk or confront anyone; he was very passive. And now Jacob passively listens to his mother instead of confronting her or at least choosing another course of action. It is also obvious that Abraham and Sarah did not talk to one another. Isaac and Rebekah did not talk. It stands to reason, then, that Jacob and his wife would be plagued with the same sickness.

Let's look again at these three patterns:

Don't trust. All through these stories, there is an unhealthy trust. Abraham, Isaac, and Jacob didn't trust those they should have trusted, and they trusted those they should not have trusted.

- Abraham didn't trust God.
- Sarah didn't trust Abraham.
- Isaac didn't trust God.
- Rebekah and Jacob didn't trust Isaac.
- Jacob should have trusted God, the prophecies, and his father, but he didn't.
- Jacob should not have trusted his mother, but he did.
- Esau didn't trust anybody.

Don't talk. Neither Isaac, Rebekah, Jacob, nor Esau talked about what was going on. Family secrets are a dead giveaway to codependency or family sin. The power of family sin lies in its secrecy. The way to rob family sin of its power is to talk about it with someone who is compassionate and trustworthy. If you don't share with another person, at least talk about it to God in prayer.

Don't feel. All through these stories there is an amazing absence of feeling. There is almost no feeling of remorse or repentance over sin committed against another person. Neither Rebekah nor Jacob seem to feel the impact or damage of their actions. There is almost no reporting of people coming face-to-face with their feelings and sharing those feelings with another, stopping an action, or learning from an action. The characters think, speak, take actions, and experience personal pain as a result of those actions, but there is very little explanation of their feelings.

Our inability to come face-to-face with what we feel could lead to actions that are sinful, heartless, and cruel.

3. The answer to family sin in each of the passages we have studied is God's forgiveness. God's forgiveness will prevent a lot of family mess. Before we will seek forgiveness, though, we must come to recognize the sins of our fathers and mothers and how they have uniquely become our sins. When you face what is going on, then you can try to begin to face why it is impacting you the way it is—and then you can ask God for forgiveness. But it is tough to ask God for forgiveness before you have acknowledged that you have done anything wrong.

People today do nothing wrong. Have you ever noticed that? They say *if*: "If I have done anything to you, please forgive me" or "If I have sinned…" or "If I have hurt you…" What's the *if* for? I've just told you that you did hurt me, so where's that *if* coming from?

They don't want to admit that they've done anything wrong; they want to leave it hanging there like a question. "Well, maybe I did something wrong and maybe I didn't. *If* you can prove that I did it, then I'm sorry." Let's change the *if* to *since*, all right? "Since I hurt you and made a mess of this situation through my sin, I'm asking you to forgive me."

4. We will see in the next chapter that God used this family mess to separate Jacob unto Himself. Jacob had to be sent to a far country for some learning experiences. After these experiences, God would bring Jacob back home. On his way back home, God wrestled with Jacob, changed his name to Israel, and extended the promises of Abraham and Isaac to him.

5. All through our study of the history of the family of Abraham, we can see God's grace. God works beneath, behind, through, and beyond family mess to establish His covenant promises to this family. As soon as Jacob left home, God gave him the dream of the ladder ascending into heaven and reaffirmed His covenant with him—the covenant of Isaac and Abraham.

By the way, did you notice that God didn't reaffirm His covenant with Jacob until he had left home? Sometimes God has to get us away from people so that He can bring us back home a changed person.

As we become more and more aware of the family sin and family mess in the line of Abraham, Isaac, and Jacob, it is all the more remarkable to hear God say, *"I am the God of Abraham, Isaac, and Jacob."* With all of their family mess, He was still pleased to be identified with them and say He's their God.

That brings hope to me. If God worked it out for them, He'll work it out for you and me!

DISCUSSION QUESTIONS

1. Are you aware of anything that you have deeply longed for from your father?

2. If you are aware of a deep longing, what have you done to try to get that longing filled by your father? If he is deceased, does that longing now impact you in another way?

3. What do you feel about the fatherhood of God and His ability to fill your deep longing?

4. Are you in competition with a sibling or another person as you pursue your own identity?

5. How has this competition hurt you and how do you think forgiveness can help you?

CHAPTER 9

Wrestling Your Way Out of Family Mess
(The Guiding Light, Part 2)

In this chapter we are going to once again see God work beneath, behind, through and beyond family mess to establish His covenant and promises to Jacob. But before we get to our text, we need just a little background.

It is interesting to me that it says this in Genesis 29:1: *"Then Jacob went on his journey, and came to the land of the sons of the east."* We know that east represents the way of the world. When Jacob chose to listen to his mother, he chose a path that eventually led him away from the Promised Land and toward the way of the world. When we choose to listen to anyone instead of the Word of God we choose to leave the Promised Land of abundant Christian living for the way of the world!

After his journey, Jacob settled with Laban, Rebekah's brother, and worked for him for many years. As we take a short look at the relationship between Laban and Jacob, we can see that Rebekah was very much like her brother. Their own family's mess had deeply impacted both of them.

Let's look at the relationship between Laban and Jacob. Laban tricked Jacob repeatedly during his stay. The biggest trick involved Laban's daughter, Rachel, whom Jacob loved.

Jacob arranged with Laban to pay Rachel's dowry price by giving him seven years of labor. But at the end of that time, Laban tricked Jacob and sent Rachel's older sister, Leah, into the wedding tent instead. Jacob didn't realize the switch until morning.

I know that sounds confusing. How could this man have sex with somebody and not know who it was? For one thing, it was dark. There were no electric lights. All they had were candles and oil lamps. For another thing, women in that day (unlike women of today) were covered up in every possible way, including a veil over their face. She was covered all through the wedding and covered still at night.

So it was dark and she was covered. Plus, it was after a night of festivities and a lot of drinking when Leah came into the tent. So no wonder Jacob didn't figure it out until the morning light appeared. All of a sudden, there in the place of the woman he expected to find was Leah. It's very funny to us, I'm sure, but it wasn't funny to him.

When he confronted Laban, Laban told Jacob of the custom of the older daughter marrying before the younger daughter. He said he could have Rachel if he agreed to seven *more* years of labor. Jacob was trapped because he loved Rachel. So he worked fourteen years for her. This is also a touching love story, isn't it?

All told, Jacob worked for Laban twenty years: fourteen years for his two daughters and six years for his flock. Over the course of his employment, Laban changed his wages ten times. Now we see where Rebekah's family mess comes from.

This is the outcome of trying to trick out of relatives something that only God can give to us. We end up losing the promised land of abundant Christian living *and* we end up living down in the world with sinners who will trick us on every hand.

But there is another statement that puts the exclamation point on all that had happened: *"Yet your father has cheated me and changed my wages ten times; however, God did not allow him to hurt me"* (Genesis 31:7). Jacob could see that God had overruled ten wage changes and twenty years of family mess!

Now here is a powerful truth that we all need to get in touch with: When God is for you and has a destiny for you, He will not allow family mess to ultimately hurt you. There is no weapon formed against you that can prosper! In spite of all that Jacob had done, God did not abandon him. Once again, he received "the guiding light" of God. *"Then the Lord said to Jacob, 'Return to the land of your fathers and to your relatives, and I will be with you'"* (Genesis 31:3).

Sometimes God separates us from our relatives because His high calling in our lives demands total separation. This is what

He did with Abraham. But sometimes God separates us from our relatives because His high calling demands that He prepare us to go back and minister to our relatives.

Did you get that? Many people can be secretly delighted to be separated from relatives that they don't like or who bring family mess into their lives. Well, God didn't separate you from them because of your likes and dislikes. He didn't separate you because of your will, but because of His will. He might want you to go back to them.

That's what He wanted from Jacob. So Jacob gathered up his wives, his children, and all the livestock that the Lord had blessed him with, and he journeyed back to Canaan, the Promised Land—the land of his destiny.

But even as Jacob left Laban's home, more family mess happened. When they left, Jacob left without telling Laban. As they left, Rachel stole the household idols. Now you will see that I was not just guessing when I wrote that Abraham's father and family were probably idol worshipers: Laban had household idols.

You are probably thinking, "But that is Rebekah's family line, not Abraham's!" Well, watch this. Laban's father was Bethuel, and Bethuel's father was Nahor, and Nahor was *Abraham's brother.* So Laban is the grandson of Abraham's brother. Chances are, Abraham would have had household gods, too, had it not been for the grace of God!

Can you imagine what you might still have leftover from your own family mess were it not for the grace of God? The next time you look at your family and say, "I don't know what's wrong with those people," just remember that but for the grace of God you would be just like them. God has delivered you and lifted you out because there is something He wants to do with you. But without God, you would be just like those people. So praise God and judge not.

When Laban discovered that Jacob was gone and his household gods were missing, he pursued Jacob to recover them. When he overtook Jacob he asked him why he deceived him by leaving secretly and not giving him the opportunity to kiss his sons and daughters and send them away with joy, and he accused Jacob of stealing his gods.

You can tell by Laban's language that he was not concerned with kissing his relatives or sending them away with joy, because he was still referring to them as *his*.

Here's something else to think about: It's sad when you have a god that someone can steal! If you worship anything that can be taken away—like a house, car, a piece of furniture, money, health, good looks, or another person—then you're just asking for trouble and your house is built on sinking sand.

Jacob told Laban the truth. He told him that he was afraid that Laban would take his daughters from him by force. He told him to search their belongings, saying that whoever was found with the gods would die. He was not aware that Rachel had stolen the gods. Laban could not find the idols, because Rachel sat on them and used the excuse of being on her period for not getting up. Family mess! Rachel had learned deception well from her father.

So Jacob journeyed on. As he approached his home, he sent messengers to Esau to see if he was still angry, and he set up camp and prayed. His prayer is worth repeating.

> O God of my father Abraham and God of my father Isaac, O LORD, who said to me, 'Return to your country and to your relatives, and I will prosper you,' I am unworthy of all the lovingkindness and of all the faithfulness which You have shown to Your servant; for with my staff only I crossed this Jordan, and now I have become two companies.
>
> Deliver me, I pray, from the hand of my brother, from the hand of Esau; for I fear him, that he will come and attack me and the mothers with the children. For You said, 'I will surely prosper you and make your descendants as the sand of the sea, which is too great to be numbered' (Genesis 32:9–12).

Let's notice a few things about this prayer:

- He addressed God as the God of Abraham and Isaac, and as Yahweh (or Jehovah).

- He acknowledged his unworthiness.

- He acknowledged God's physical blessings.

- He asked for protection from Esau. (Notice that the "give me" part didn't start until way down in the prayer. We *start* with, "Lord, give me… I need… You know that Your child needs…" But there are some things we ought to address before we get down there!)

- He reminded God of His covenant promise.

Then Jacob divided his family into two groups. He thought, "If Esau is still angry and attacks, one of the two groups will be able to escape."

All right, all of that is background for the text I want to talk about in this chapter. It's in Genesis 32:

> Now he arose that same night and took his two wives and his two maids and his eleven children, and crossed the ford of the Jabbok. He took them and sent them across the stream. And he sent across whatever he had.
>
> Then Jacob was left alone, and a man wrestled with him until daybreak. When he saw that he had not prevailed against him, he touched the socket of his thigh; so the socket of Jacob's thigh was dislocated while he wrestled with him.

Then he said, "Let me go, for the dawn is breaking." But he said, "I will not let you go unless you bless me." So he said to him, "What is your name?" And he said, "Jacob." He said, "Your name shall no longer be Jacob, but Israel; for you have striven with God and with men and have prevailed."

Then Jacob asked him and said, "Please tell me your name." But he said, "Why is it that you ask my name?" And he blessed him there.

So Jacob named the place Peniel, for he said, "I have seen God face to face, yet my life has been preserved."

Now the sun rose upon him just as he crossed over Penuel, and he was limping on his thigh. Therefore, to this day the sons of Israel do not eat the sinew of the hip which is on the socket of the thigh, because he touched the socket of Jacob's thigh in the sinew of the hip (Genesis 32:22–32).

Let me point out some things from this story as they relate to family mess:

1. God wrestled with Jacob to deliver him from family mess. It was not Jacob who challenged God to a wrestling match, but God who engaged Jacob. If it were Jacob wrestling with someone, he might be trying to gain something from that man. But here it appears that the man was trying to gain something from Jacob. I believe the thing God was after here was to bring Jacob to see what a poor, feeble, worthless creature he was. *God wanted to bring Jacob to the end of himself.*

God has a purpose in wrestling with us. He wants to bring us to the dawning of a new day, but He can only do that by bringing us to the end of ourselves. Sometimes He puts us in a submission hold—He's not asking us to say *uncle* but *Jesus!* But we struggle for a blessing; we struggle to hold on to ourselves. We must learn to give in and say, "Jesus! You are the Lord and Master of my life."

Family mess will bring you to the end of yourself. It will bring you to the point where you say, "There isn't anything I can do with my mother!" Family mess will bring you to the point where you recognize there is nothing you can do with your children or your aunt and uncle or spouse. There is nothing I can do with these people. They are in God's hands! They're there anyway, but sometimes He has to use family mess to make us realize it and let go.

"In countless scenarios, each one of us will stay the way we are until something forces us to change—perhaps a crisis, God, or both. We won't make the hard choices until we have to."[1] In Jacob's case, it was both. God had brought Jacob to the point where he recognized there was nothing he could do about his situation. His mother had messed him up, his father had let it happen, his brother was out to murder him—and there was nothing he could do about any of it.

God often uses crises of family mess to change us and call us to our higher walk. He will call us out of that family mess. He will call us out of that divorce. He will call us out of those relatives who don't like us. He will call us out of those things to come on up a little bit higher. Let family mess work its work.

2. God wrestled with Jacob until daybreak. "The reference to dawn indicates that his struggle continued for a good while."[2] God is a patient Wrestler. He doesn't mind wrestling with us until He can effect the dawning of a new day in our lives. This match is not the best two out of three falls, and there are no time limits. He wants to bring us out of the night of death to a morning of resurrection. God wants to raise us to new life out of the death of family mess!

Do you want to be delivered from family mess? If you don't want to be delivered, there is no use in me talking about it. Is that a strange question? Doesn't everybody want to be delivered? No they don't.

That is why Jesus asked the man at the pool at Siloam, "Do you wish to be here?" Every time the water is troubled you sit there and say, "I don't have anybody to put me in." Is it about putting you in or is it about getting into the water? If it is about getting into the water, then when you think the pool is about to be troubled, start crawling and doing anything you can to get into that water to get a healing. If you want to be healed, you don't sit there and complain about there not being anybody to put you in the water. So I'll ask you the same question Jesus asked: Do you want to be made whole?

Some of us want to end our wrestling match with God by avoiding our families. We think that's how we can avoid family mess. But God allows and uses family mess because He is wrestling to bring about the dawning of a new day in our lives. We don't have to live in the death of family mess when we have the promise of Jehovah God.

3. God wrestled with Jacob until the socket of his thigh was dislocated. "When Jacob wrestled against God's divine dealing with him, 'God touched the hollow of his thigh; and the hollow of Jacob's thigh was out of joint as He wrestled with him.' The sentence of death had to be written on the flesh."[3]

- God wrestled with Jacob until his flesh was crucified.

- God wrestled with Jacob until the genetic source of his family mess was broken.

- Jacob had to have his flesh broken.

- He had to have his gene pool broken.

- He had to have his family sin broken.

Likewise, for Jesus to deliver us from our family mess:

- We must have our flesh crucified.

- We must have our dependence upon our genetic heritage broken.

- We must experience brokenness.

- We must have the sin of our gene pool—the image of our father—broken.

- We must have our family sin broken.

There comes a point in Christianity when God will kick everything away from you—all your friends, all your staff, all your crutches, everything that you ever depended upon, everything that you thought was going to hold you up. God will kick it out from under you because you've got to come to a point where you depend solely upon Him. Praise God for the end result, even though during the process it doesn't feel very nice.

"Jacob carried the marks of this encounter with him all his life, in the dislocation of his thigh.... By the dislocation of his thigh the carnal nature of his previous wrestling was declared to be powerless and wrong."[4] For the rest of his days, Jacob had a built-in reminder that the flesh can never accomplish what only the Spirit can bring to pass.

We need the power of our flesh dislocated. We need the power of our carnal natures dislocated. We need the brokenness of our flesh as a reminder that we can never wrestle out of relatives or accomplish in our own power that which only the Spirit can bring to pass!

Most Christians haven't found this out yet. They haven't found it out yet because they are still trying to walk in their own power, walk in their own accord, straighten out their own messes, and work through their own trouble. Maybe that's you, too. You don't recognize that you are crippled and you can't do it. You need to be picked up by the power of the Holy Spirit and carried in the arms of Jesus Christ. You need to let Him work it out for you down in your family where you thought things could never get worked out. Jesus can move in and do some powerful things in there.

4. God wrestled with Jacob to change his name. In ancient Jewish culture one's name represented one's character. The name that Jacob received from his family meant one who grasps the heel of another, supplanter, cheater. But God gave him a new family name, representative of who he was in the family of God. His new name was Israel, which means "he fights or persists with God."

Although it was God who engaged Jacob, Jacob wrestled with God and man and he prevailed. It seems that he prevailed with God in prayer. Hosea seems to state this:

> In the womb he took his brother by the heel, and in his maturity he contended with God. Yes, he wrestled with the angel and prevailed; he wept and sought His favor (Hosea 12:3–4a).

The phrase *sought His favor* is the Hebrew word *chanan*. It means "to pray or make supplication." The point is this: One of the major ways to overcome family mess is to wrestle it into submission through the spiritual discipline of prayer. Prevail upon God in prayer to deliver you from family mess. And when you prevail upon God in prayer and God crucifies your reliance upon your flesh and your family, God gives you a new name, which represents who you are in Him.

- You are no longer called a sinner, but a saint.
- You are no longer called a slave, but a friend.
- You are no longer called an acquaintance, but a brother or sister.
- You are no longer called a laborer, but a priest and king or queen.
- You are no longer called a guest of the wedding, but the Bride of Christ.

5. God wrestled with Jacob until He blessed him. He blessed Jacob with the covenant promises of Abraham and Isaac. He blessed Jacob with a new name, which represented a major change in the life of Jacob. He blessed Jacob to return to the land of his birth, the Promised Land. And there were more blessings to come.

But God couldn't or wouldn't give Jacob the blessings He still had in store for him until He and Jacob had wrestled the family mess into submission.

God *used* family mess in the life of Jacob in the following ways:

- He sent him away from home that He might bring him back home.

- He left home running for his life; he returned home with the promise of his life.

- He left home to follow the course of the world; he returned by the prophecy of God.

- He left the Promised Land not understanding what he had; he returned with God's assurance that the land was his.

- He left home empty; he came back full.

- He left home with no fellowship with God; he came back having experienced the intimacy of wrestling with God.

- He left home with a name that meant "cheater"; he came back with a name that meant "one who has prevailed with God."

- He left home confused; he came back certain of his destiny.

- He left home immature, frightened, and passive; he came back experienced, confident, and assertive.

- He left home because of family mess; he returned having conquered it.

God is going to engage us in a big-time wrestling match until He crushes the flesh of our family mess and we wrestle our family mess into submission!

DISCUSSION QUESTIONS

1. Describe your big-time wrestling match with God.

2. Who is winning?

3. In what ways has God crippled you and what does that mean to you?

4. In what ways has God changed your name and what does that mean to you?

5. What family member is God preparing you to minister to?

CHAPTER 10

Roots: Part 1
(All in the Family)

Jacob inherited a double measure of family mess. It came from both sides of his family. Allow me to trace out the confluence of these two streams of family mess that joined together to negatively impact Jacob's life. Let's look at the "Roots" of family mess in the life of Jacob—"The Young and the Restless."

First, from his father's side of the family:

- Jacob's great-grandfather, Terah, was an idol worshiper.
- His grandfather, Abraham, was a passive man who had trouble trusting God.
- His father, Isaac, was a passive man who had trouble trusting God.
- Jacob himself was a passive man who had trouble trusting God.
- Abraham was a worshiper of idols, but he was delivered by the grace of God.

Now let's look at the family mess Jacob inherited from his mother's side:

- Jacob's grandfather on his mother's side, Nahor, was an idol worshiper. (This is Rebekah's father, Abraham's brother, and is not to be confused with Abraham's grandfather, who was also named Nahor.)
- Since Rebekah's grandfather, father, and brother were all idol worshipers, it is likely that Rebekah was an idol worshiper, too.
- Jacob's wives, Rachel and Leah (who were Laban's daughters and thus from his mother Rebekah's side of the family), worshiped idols.
- Later, as we will see in this chapter, idol worship manifested itself as a stronghold sin in Jacob's household.
- Jacob's mother, Rebekah, and her brother, Laban, were both tricksters, which leads us to believe that their father, Nahor, may also have been a trickster.
- Jacob's wife, Rachel, Laban's daughter, was also a trickster who coveted and stole her father's household gods.

The joint influence of both sides of the family impacted Jacob greatly. Naturally and genetically, Jacob was inclined to be a passive trickster who had trouble trusting God and gravitated toward idol worship.

You need to become aware of the mighty river of family mess that has converged in you from the two streams of your family. Take a deep look at your "Roots" to see what you have inherited.

When we get through feeling the impact of the river of family mess and examining our roots, I think we will come to the conclusion that many of the things we are facing are "All in the Family"!

- Alcoholism—"All In The Family"
- Anger—"All In The Family"
- Chronic depression—"All In The Family"
- Negativity—"All In The Family"
- Passivity—"All In The Family"
- Relationship addictions—"All In The Family"
- Physical abuse—"All In The Family"
- Sexual abuse—"All In The Family"
- Sexual idolatry—"All In The Family"
- Substance abuse—"All In The Family"

One of the most curious things about many Christians I know is their ability to see the deep mess of their family and yet believe that it did not impact them. "Oh, yes, there is some deep family mess in my family. I'm so glad it skipped my generation." I've got news for you: It *didn't* skip your generation. You might be able to rise above family mess by the grace of God, but you are a part of the stream of family mess in your family. Don't be deceived: The family mess you have inherited will impact you in some way.

Back to Jacob. In spite of the great family mess that flowed to and through Jacob, there was still great hope for him. That hope lay in the words of Jehovah: "I am the God of Abraham, Isaac, *and Jacob.*"

Jehovah God worked through all of this genetic and family mess to give Jacob the covenant promises and destiny that He had ordained for Him. Jacob's roots did not stop God from blessing him. The family mess Jacob inherited did not hinder God from bringing about his destiny.

If God would do this for Jacob, He will do it for you. Your roots need not disqualify you from the blessings of Jehovah God. This is great news! When you accept Christ as your personal Savior, you are engrafted into Him. You become a part of a new tree with a new root system. Notice with me:

- Jesus is the root of Jesse who grew up out of dry ground.
- Jesus is the green tree of Jehovah God.
- Jesus is the tree of life whose leaves are good for the healing of the nations.
- Jesus is the tree that is planted by the rivers of water, whose leaves and fruit do not wither.
- Jesus is the vine and we are the branches, and we receive the flow of life, joy, and blessings from Him.

We have now followed the iniquity of Abraham down through the third generation—Jacob. But our key verse says that God visits the iniquity of the fathers on the children to the third and fourth generations. We are finally ready to move on to the fourth generation to see how the consequences of Abraham's sins play themselves out.

Let's jump back to the time before Jacob left Laban's home to return to the Promised Land. Rachel, his best-loved wife, could not have children. As we have seen, in Bible times that was the worst possible plight of a woman. Yet God opened the womb of Leah, the less-loved wife. That seems like poetic justice to me: The one who is less honored by man receives the greater blessing from God.

When Rachel saw that she couldn't have children, she gave Jacob her handmaid, Bilhah, as a surrogate mother. But in due time God blessed Rachel to have children. Not surprisingly, her two sons became the ones best loved by Jacob.

In the meantime, Leah had stopped having children. So she did what Rachel had done: She gave Jacob her handmaid, Zilpah, as a surrogate mother. Jacob had two wives, two surrogate mothers, a total of twelve sons, and one daughter. Family mess and "All My Children"!

We have already seen this handmaid scenario in the life of Abraham and Sarah. But here it is doubled. That which is tolerated by one generation is accepted by the next, and that which is accepted by one generation is embraced by the next. You see, when we don't stop the family mess, when we don't stop the lying or the addictions or the anger, it only gets worse. Each generation gets a little farther away.

So, what kind of impact do you think this whole situation had upon Jacob's children? I believe that they were certainly aware of this whole mess, and it had to have had a negative impact upon them.

But even if this didn't impact the children negatively, there was another scenario that almost certainly involved them in family mess. This story involves Reuben, Leah's firstborn.

> Now in the days of wheat harvest Reuben went and found mandrakes in the field, and brought them to his mother Leah. Then Rachel said to Leah, "Please give me some of your son's mandrakes."
>
> But she said to her, "Is it a small matter for you to take my husband? And would you take my son's mandrakes also?" So Rachel said, "Therefore he may lie with you tonight in return for your son's mandrakes."
>
> When Jacob came in from the field in the evening, then Leah went out to meet him and said, "You must come in to me, for I have surely hired you with my son's mandrakes." So he lay with her that night. (Genesis 30:14–16)

What a mess! Two women bargaining for the sexual favors of their husband, using their children's goods as bargaining chips.

A mandrake was a small, perennial plant native to the Middle East. Although not grown for food, its root and berries are edible. The Ancient Near East viewed it as an aphrodisiac and fertility drug. An aphrodisiac is something that arouses or increases sexual desire. It is often called a love apple or devil's apple. Since these women were basically vying to have the most children, the mandrakes would be seen as a competitive edge. No wonder Rachel wanted them. And no wonder Leah used them to advance her chances of fertility. In such a situation, we have to imagine that the children would be caught in the middle of this family mess.

Rachel and Leah were probably using the children to communicate to one another. I can see them sending their children back and forth with messages and mandrakes. This is called *triangulation,* and it is a symptom of dysfunctionality. Triangulation is learned in childhood. It gives the child a sense of power to be included and involved in the lives of others. But sometimes that involvement can backfire and both parties can get angry with him or her. Triangulation can also become emotionally exhausting and frustrating.

What does triangulation look like? Parents using children to carry messages like: "Tell your mother I'm angry with her," "Tell your father I'm not going out tonight," "Tell your mother to go to the doctor," and "Tell your father to get a new suit."

Did your parents do this to you? If so, recognize it. And don't do it to your children!

If only this were all the family mess in Jacob's family. But it isn't. In the thirty-fourth chapter of Genesis, we come to a very sordid story. The passage is too long to include, so let me relate it to you.

The incident takes place in Shechem, which was a city in Canaan, and with the sons of Hamor. Shechem, the son of Hamor the Hivite, raped Dinah, the daughter of Jacob and Leah. Yet Shechem was still deeply attracted to Dinah and loved her, so he asked his father to get Dinah for him to be his wife. When Dinah's brothers heard what had happened they were very angry.

Hamor spoke to Jacob about arranging a marriage, and then he talked to Dinah's brothers. Hamor proposed a treaty that would join their two peoples as one. But because Dinah's brothers were angry, they lied to Hamor. They said, "We will accept the conditions of your treaty, if you and all your people will agree to be circumcised. If you won't agree to be circumcised, we cannot possibly accept the terms of your agreement."

The request seemed reasonable to Hamor and Shechem, so Shechem did not delay in meeting the terms of the agreement because he delighted in Dinah.

Since Shechem was more respected than all of his father's household, he and his father went to the city gates and presented the proposal to the men of the city. They told them, "We can prosper in a number of ways if we unite with this people: We can intermarry with them and trade with them—and they have much livestock. But there is one condition: We must be circumcised!" Believe it or not, all of the men of the city agreed and were circumcised.

Now comes the sneaky part. On the third day after their

circumcision, when all the men of the city were incapacitated from pain, Simeon and Levi (two of Dinah's brothers) sneaked up on the city and killed every man with swords.

The sin we saw in Abraham was bad enough, but it wasn't as bad as what we saw in Isaac. But what we saw in Isaac wasn't as bad as what we saw in Jacob—which isn't as bad as what we see when we get to his sons—to the third and fourth generations.

Now the family mess of Jacob's family included murder—even genocide! I wish that were all, but there's more. To sibling rivalry and murder, we can add idol worship.

Let's jump forward in the story to a point after Jacob has returned to the Promised Land and met his brother, Esau. We know that Rachel stole her father's household gods. But now we're going to see that she didn't steal them just to have them— she stole them to worship them. It appears that idol worship continued in the household of Jacob for years, and it seems that Jacob allowed it. That would not be unusual considering that his father and grandfather were both very passive towards their wives. Notice this passage:

> Then God said to Jacob, "Arise, go up to Bethel and live there, and make an altar there to God, who appeared to you when you fled from your brother Esau."
>
> So Jacob said to his household and to all who were with him, "Put away the foreign gods which are

among you, and purify yourselves and change your garments; and let us arise and go up to Bethel, and I will make an altar there to God, who answered me in the day of my distress and has been with me wherever I have gone."

So they gave to Jacob all the foreign gods which they had and the rings which were in their ears, and Jacob hid them under the oak which was near Shechem (Genesis 35:1–4).

The earrings referred to may have been magical apparel with words engraved on them that were supposed to ward off evil. Family mess! Check your family to see if they've got any amulets or trinkets or jewelry that may have something demonic attached to them. Don't wear something like that around your neck.

These children of Jacob were a long way from worshiping God. But sibling rivalry, murder, and idol worship were not the only elements of Jacob's family mess. In the midst of all of this family mess, we also get stories implying that sexual idolatry or addiction was a problem in this family. I use the term sexual idolatry because whenever anyone is addicted to some form of sexuality, that form of sexuality becomes an idol.

We see Reuben again, this time showing that he had a problem with sexual idolatry: *"It came about while Israel was dwelling in that land, that Reuben went and lay with Bilhah his father's concubine, and Israel heard of it"* (Genesis 35:22a). Now we have to add incest to the list of sordid family mess in Jacob's family. By the way, Jacob—whom God had since renamed "Israel"— didn't confront Reuben about this. He reacted just like his father and grandfather would have—with passivity.

What about you? Are there any situations in your family in which some sexual sin was done but no one has dealt with it?

I'm sorry to say it, but there's more. Two other sexual idolatry incidents involved Judah, another one of Leah's sons. The first is that he had sex with a Canaanite woman, who produced two children. The Bible does not say that they were married, so I must assume that Judah was participating in illicit, premarital sex. The second incident is an episode when Judah used the services of what he thought was a prostitute, but who turned out to be his daughter-in-law in disguise. What a mess! Sexual idolatry, misconduct, and addiction seemed to be a stronghold in the family of Jacob.

Do you see how the sins of the fathers are coming to a head in the fourth generation of the children? What a legacy of mess. But don't miss this point, either: Despite all of it, the twelve sons of Jacob would become the twelve tribes of the Children of Israel, the people of God, the apple of God's eye. They were God's people whom He chose by grace and blessed because of His gracious promise:

> For you are a holy people to the Lord your God;
> the Lord your God has chosen you to be a people
> for His own possession out of all the peoples who

are on the face of the earth. The LORD did not set His love on you nor choose you because you were more in number than any of the peoples, for you were the fewest of all peoples, but because the LORD loved you and kept the oath which He swore to your forefathers (Deuteronomy 7:6–8a).

Regardless of the family mess in your family, if you have accepted Jesus Christ as your personal Savior, you are part of the Church, the body of Jesus Christ, the Bride of the heavenly Bridegroom, the family of God, the sons and daughters of God, who are in Christ Jesus. That ought to give you joy! That ought to give you hope. The world says, "You are nothing but an illegitimate child." But God says, "You are My Child! I died for you. I have a destiny for you, and I'm taking you somewhere where you can spend eternity with Me."

And you also have a powerful Scripture that affirms this truth:

Blessed be the God and Father of our Lord Jesus Christ, who has blessed us with every spiritual blessing in the heavenly places in Christ, just as He chose us in Him before the foundation of the world, that we would be holy and blameless before Him. In love He predestined us to adoption as sons through Jesus Christ to Himself, according to the kind intention of His will, to the praise of the glory of His grace, which He freely bestowed on us in the Beloved. *In Him we have redemption through His blood, the forgiveness of our trespasses, according to the riches of His grace which He lavished on us* (Ephesians 1:3–8a, emphasis mine).

Throughout eternal ages He will be showing you His grace, if you have believed in Him as your personal Savior. He will be pouring out His grace. He will be lavishing it upon you. You see, hope is not in the present, but it is in Jesus. Hope is in the fact that one day God shall right every wrong, straighten everything out, and give you an inheritance. Hope is in the fact that maybe you are not who you think you ought to be now, but in Jesus one day you are going to be everything He wants you to be and you will walk with Him and He will talk with you. We will spend eternity together because of what He has done in Christ!

Because of His grace He saved me. Because of His grace He lifted me up. Because of His grace He turned me around. Because of His grace He planted my feet on a rock. Because of His grace He called me to the ministry. Because of His grace He had a destiny for me. Because of His grace my name is written in the Lamb's Book of Life. Because of His grace I'll spend eternity with Him. Because of His grace I get a reward. Because of His grace I get a new name.

If that doesn't make you excited, you will never get excited. If that doesn't generate joy in your soul, you aren't ever going to get any. This ought to make you happy. Your job can't change your destiny. Your family can't change your destiny. Hard times can't change your destiny. Family mess can't change your destiny. None of these things can change what God has for you in

Heaven one day. Eyes have not seen and ears have not heard the blessing that God has prepared for those who love Him.

DISCUSSION QUESTIONS

1. When you look at the mighty rivers of your mother and father's side of your family, can you see how their family mess flows together to you?

2. Are you aware of any sins or weaknesses in you that have roots in your family history?

3. Have you or are you seeing any triangulation in your family? How has that impacted you?

4. Do you see any evidences of idolatry in your family tree?

5. How do the promises of God, which come along with salvation, help you to face the mess of your family?

CHAPTER 11

Roots: Part 2
(All My Children)

Now that we have surveyed four generations of Abraham's family, we can see how the consequences of his sin created family mess for his family all the way down to his great-grandchildren.

In light of what we have seen, let me expand our understanding of dysfunctionality and codependency.

The term *codependent* originally meant the spouse, lover, or significant other of someone who was chemically dependent.[1] But since those days, *codependency* has taken on a life and an identity of its own. Many professionals now use codependency as a diagnostic term that refers to a specific set of emotional and behavioral symptoms.[2]

One book says this:

> In its broadest sense, *codependency* can be defined

as *an addiction to people, behaviors, or things.* Co-dependency is the fallacy of trying to control interior feelings by controlling people, things, and events on the outside. To the codependent, control or lack of it is central to every aspect of life.[3]

Authors John and Linda Friel give a formal definition for codependency in their book *Adult Children: The Secrets of Dysfunctional Families:*

> Co-dependency is a dysfunctional pattern of living which emerges from our family of origin as well as our culture, producing arrested identity development, and resulting in an over-reaction to things outside of us and an under-reaction to things inside of us. Left untreated, it can deteriorate into an addiction.[4]

Psychologists have identified several symptoms connected with codependency. These include: depression, tolerance of inappropriate behavior, dulled or inappropriate emotions, self-defeating coping strategies, strong need to control self and others, stress-related physical symptoms, abuse of self, neglect of self, difficulty with intimacy and/or sexuality, fear of abandonment, shame, inappropriate guilt, eventual addictions, and rages.

These are personal characteristics, but there are also family characteristics of codependency. The dysfunctional characteristics of a family should be looked at as a line with varying degrees of seriousness. On a continuum from extremely healthy to extremely unhealthy families, you will find some or all of the following characteristics, depending on how functional or dysfunctional a family is: physical, emotional, or sexual abuse/neglect and vicarious abuse; perfectionism; rigid rules, lifestyle, and/or belief systems; the "no talk rule"—keeping "the family secrets"; inability to identify and/or express feelings; triangulation (a communication pattern using one person as intermediary); double messages/double binds; inability to play, have fun, and be spontaneous; high tolerance for inappropriate behavior/pain; and enmeshment (the inability to realize where you end and someone else begins).[5]

Some dysfunctional families have few of these characteristics. Some families have all of them.

In Abraham's family, we have covered many sordid stories. But there is one that perfectly sums up the family mess in the fourth generation after him—the story of Joseph.

You would think that Jacob would have learned something from the conditions he grew up in. He had seen the impact of parental favoritism. Perhaps he had even said to himself, "When I have a family, I will never do what my parents did!" But here is Jacob doing exactly what was done to him. The Bible tells us that Jacob loved Joseph more than all his other sons. He was just asking for family mess.

When Joseph was seventeen years old, he was pasturing Jacob's flock with his brothers. But he came home and told on his brothers. Evidently Joseph would keep an eye on his brothers while they were shepherding Jacob's herds, and then report back to his father.

That would be bad enough, but the situation was complicated by the fact that Jacob loved Joseph more than all of his sons, because he was the son of his old age—and the first son of Rachel, his favorite wife. Jacob made it worse by showing his preference for Joseph by making him a multicolored tunic. The Bible tells us that the other brothers hated Joseph for being their father's favorite. They couldn't even speak to him on friendly terms. Family mess!

Just as Jacob's father had preferred Esau over him, and his mother had preferred him to Esau, now Jacob preferred Joseph over his other sons. Jacob was passing the family mess of his father on to his own sons. His unfinished business with his father would be picked up and finished by his sons. Jacob's pain is carried by and manifested in his sons. Some of the tragic things that they do may simply be a way of seeking attention from their father. You see, when people can't get the love they need, they may settle for any attention, positive or negative.

Serious sibling rivalry is a blight on any family. It is ugly to see a child spoiled because of favoritism and another child rejected because he or she is not the favorite. Both children will carry the pain of their father deep into adulthood. The spoiled child is actually set up for some form of failure, because life will not treat that child in the same manner as the father did. And the rejected child will probably search for love and acceptance for the rest of his or her life.

Let me give you a word of advice if you are a parent with more than one child. Each child is different and must be related to differently and loved differently. I believe it is impossible to love two children equally, because they are not equal. Each child is a unique gift from God. But you must do all that you can to keep from preferring or showing a preference for one child over another.

Although you cannot love each child exactly the same or in exactly the same way, you *can* love each child *to the same extent*. You can go to the same lengths for each child. I am not sure how well I did with my children, but I at least tried to go to the same lengths for each of them.

I tried to go to both of their events, although their events were different. I tried to spend money on things that were important to them, although those things were drastically different. I tried to spend time with each of them—doing what each wanted to do.

Are you getting the picture? Are you doing this with your children? Did your parents do this with you? If they showed preference, you're probably inclined to show preference among your children. And you're probably still hurting. If this is you, examine your background. It is worth the pain of examining it and wrestling your way out of family mess to stop this pain from being passed on to your children.

All right, back to Joseph. About this time, Joseph had a dream. The dream was about his destiny. It was in keeping with the destiny that flowed through Abraham, Isaac, and Jacob. The dream seemed to be prophesying Joseph's rise to a place of authority and prominence in the world, a place from which his brothers would have to bow down to him.

Joseph didn't keep the dream to himself. He told his brothers. Family mess! Although there is little negative information about Joseph in the Bible, he did not escape the family mess of his family. The impact of family mess on Joseph is illustrated right here. Joseph seemed to flaunt the favoritism of his father in the faces of his brothers.

He wore that coat of many colors with pride. He seemed oblivious to the impact of his actions upon his brothers. Instead of holding it until Friday night at the bar mitzvah, he came out with that leather coat with all those colors. He sashayed in front of his brothers. If you have siblings, you know what he probably said: "I've got something you don't have!"

He told them the dream without regard to its impact upon their feelings. It does not seem that the dream was for them. It was for him. The dream was God telling him, "I'm going to do something for you." But he had to go out and tell everybody else.

No, Joseph didn't escape the family mess in his family. But by the grace of God, he did rise above it!

This story doesn't show us only Joseph's family mess—it shows us the mess in his brothers, too. When his brothers heard the dream, they hated him even more. Family mess! They hated their own brother. How many of us hate our own relatives? Maybe you'd better not answer that.

Then Joseph had another dream. This time the dream seemed to indicate that not only his brothers but his father and mother would one day have to bow down before him. He again shared it with his brothers, and they hated him even more. More family mess!

Finally Joseph decided to tell his parents about this dream. Now it wasn't only his brothers hating him, now his father had to rebuke him. The prophecy, which told of the destiny God had for Joseph, did not bring encouragement, happiness, or affirmation—at first. The dream brought him loneliness, misunderstanding, hatred, mistreatment, rebuke, and jealousy from his family members.

Likewise, Satan uses family mess, loneliness, misunderstanding, hatred, mistreatment, rebuke, and jealousy to discourage the prophecy, promise, and destiny of God in our lives. He has us think: "If my own mother doesn't like me, then who could love me? If my own father won't take time with me, then who can love me? If my own people think this way about me, then who can love me?"

The question you need to take into consideration is not, "What do people think about me?" but "What does God think about me?" In order to know what God thinks about you, you've got to read some of what God thinks so you can find out what He thinks about you. You'll find it in His Word. What "they" think about you will not determine your destiny—unless you let it.

But even though Jacob, now called Israel, was upset by the dream, the Bible tells us that he kept it in mind. He thought about it. He didn't altogether dismiss it. His age and experience with God would not let him completely discount it.

When your children tell you something that God is saying to them, listen and encourage them, even if you don't like the sound of it right away.

Over the course of my childhood, God showed me things that He would do in the future. I shared those with my parents, and thank God they listened to me and encouraged me. I said, "Look, the Lord is showing me preaching to all kinds of people." Thank God they said, "We affirm that. We believe in that. If God is showing you that, move towards that!" What would have happened if they had rebuked me?

After this, Joseph's brothers went to pasture their father's flock in Shechem. After a while, Jacob sent Joseph to check on the welfare of his brothers. When they saw Joseph from a distance, they plotted together to put him to death. "Here comes that dreamer!" There has already been murder in this generation, but now these boys want to murder their own brother. Family mess!

As an aside, I wonder how many times we murder our family members with our mouths? *"Death and life are in the power of the tongue"* (Proverbs 18:21a). When you're not with them, do you murder their influence and authority and character with your tongue?

But Reuben heard them plotting Joseph's murder and rescued him from their hands. Reuben told them not to kill him, but to merely throw him in a pit. Reuben was planning to pull Joseph out of the pit later and return him to his father.

When God is on our side, He orders our steps and protects us from danger—seen and unseen. When God is on our side, He makes even our enemies to be at peace with us!

So the other brothers pounced on Joseph when he reached them. They stripped him of his special coat and threw him in an empty cistern. But here's where Reuben's plan went wrong. As the brothers sat down to eat, they saw a caravan of Ishmaelites on their way to Egypt. Judah said to his brothers, "Let's not kill him. He is our own flesh and blood, after all. No, let's sell him."

The other brothers thought it was a good idea, so they pulled Joseph out of the pit and sold him into slavery for twenty pieces of silver. They sold their own brother into slavery, and those traders took Joseph to Egypt. Family mess!

Evidently, Reuben was away from the camp for some reason. When Reuben returned, he went to the pit, only to discover that Joseph was not there. He tore his clothes, a sign of grief and mourning. When he went to his brothers, they came up with the plan for what to tell their father.

Then they took Joseph's special coat, killed a male goat, dipped the coat in the blood and showed it to Jacob. They asked Jacob to identify the coat, and of course he identified it as Joseph's. From then on he assumed that Joseph had been killed. This turn of events sent Jacob into deep grief and mourning, but none of the brothers ever felt sorry enough for their father to tell him what had happened! Codependency, dysfunctionality, family sin, and family mess!

I see families all around me who could relieve the suffering of a family member with just a word—but no one will do it. Just one word of caution would make the difference. Just one word of mercy, one "here's what happened to me," one word of encouragement, one word of what happened that dark night thirty years ago, but nobody will say a word.

Meanwhile, in Egypt, Joseph was sold to Potiphar, the captain of the Pharaoh's bodyguards.

Family mess runs all through the roots of this family from Abraham to Isaac to Jacob, and especially through Jacob's sons. No doubt Jacob could see the struggle among his boys. I can imagine him sighing and, saying, "Oh, all my children!" But because Jacob didn't completely dismiss what Joseph had said about his dreams, we get a tip-off that God is at work, behind, beneath, through, above, and beyond all of this family mess. God is not through with Joseph yet.

Examine your history. Check out your roots. Find out what happened in your family that nobody wants to talk about. Whatever it is, it is still impacting you today. Sweeping family mess under the rug doesn't get rid of it. It just hides it until it starts to stink even more. Ignoring the roots of family mess doesn't get rid of it. It will simply sprout up in another place.

Uncover the family mess in your family and put it in the hands of Jesus, knowing that if God sends you to Egypt it is because He is working out His promise, prophecy, and destiny in your life.

Sooner or later, every one of us is going to come to a situation where we are sent down into Egypt where our family members seem to forsake us and everybody around us says, "You are no good," and they sell us out.

When that happens to you, recognize that if God sends you to Egypt, He's got a reason for doing it. If God sends you to Egypt, it is because He has a destiny for you down in Egypt and He has to get you there somehow. Therefore, no matter what I go through and no matter what I say, I have a destiny that I know I shall fulfill. I have a destiny in that city on the hill. I have a destiny, and it is in Jesus Christ.

I've got a destiny and it is in God's Hands. Satan may want to thwart it. He may want to tear it up and depress me, but I recognize on my way down to Egypt that there is a destiny for me. I recognize down in Paddan-aram that there is a destiny for me. I recognized when they threw me back in prison that it

wasn't over until God says it is over. It hasn't got anything to do
with a fat lady singing, but it has a lot to do with a whole lot of
Christians praising God. It is not over until God says it is over.
And God is not going to say it is over until He brings you to
where He wants you to be.

Family mess can't thwart the destiny of God. Hatred can't thwart
the destiny of God. Sexual abuse can't thwart the destiny of
God. Neglect can't thwart the destiny of God. Depression can't
stop what God wants to do in your life. Praise God!

DISCUSSION QUESTIONS

1. Explain dysfunctionality and codependency in your own words.

2. On the continuum of dysfunctionality, where do you consider your own family?

3. If you have children or siblings, can you relate to Joseph? If you don't have any children or siblings, have you experienced rivalry with some other person?

4. If you can relate to Joseph's Egypt experience, please share from that perspective.

5. How are your family roots still impacting you?

CHAPTER 12

God Is Greater than Family Mess
(The Bold and the Beautiful)

Family mess pervades the family of Abraham down to the fourth generation. Jacob's children had it in full measure. Yet God's promise to Abraham persists to the fourth generation, too, and beyond, all the way to the birth of Jesus Christ.

Let's just look at Jacob's son, Judah. He had illicit sex with a Canaanite woman, and thus produced two illegitimate children. He acted with a lack of integrity toward his daughter-in-law, Tamar. He promised to give her to one of his sons, but he didn't keep his promise. Then he had sex with someone he thought was a prostitute, but who turned out to be his daughter-in-law, Tamar, in disguise, who tricked him because he broke his word. Family mess!

In spite of these shortcomings, when Jacob gave his final prophecy and blessing to his sons, he gave a tremendous blessing to Judah:

> The scepter shall not depart from Judah, nor the ruler's staff from between his feet, until Shiloh comes, and to him shall be the obedience of the people (Genesis 49:10).

Shiloh is a proper name, generally understood by Christian scholars to be a messianic designation of Jesus Christ. Therefore Jacob was prophesying that Judah's destiny was to be a forefather of Jesus Christ.

In the last chapter, we saw Jacob's sons kidnapping their own brother, Joseph, with the intent to murder him. But, by the divine providence of God, they were prevented from murdering their own brother, and instead sold him into slavery. Family mess! We ended that chapter with Joseph being sold to Potiphar, an Egyptian official who was captain of Pharaoh's bodyguards.

Would this be the end of the story? Would the promises of God end with the fourth generation of Abraham dying in slavery? Will family mess win out in the end? Sounds like a Batman episode, doesn't it? What will happen to the Caped Crusaders? Will Batman and Robin be stumped by the Riddler? Is this the end of the Dynamic Duo?

I am glad that I can emphatically answer no! All through this book we have seen God working beneath, behind, through, in spite of, above, and beyond family mess. So we know He's going to work this situation out. But how?

Well, let's find out. The Bible tells us that, *"The LORD was with*

Joseph, so he became a successful man" (Genesis 39:2a). Potiphar saw how the Lord caused everything that Joseph did to prosper. Note that God's blessings were upon Joseph, even though his legacy of family mess was prominent and long.

Is the Lord with you? If He is, He will make you successful—according to His definition of success. I have seen this periodically: A man or woman with a great legacy of family mess will overcome that legacy by the grace and power of Jesus Christ. By every right, this man or woman should be in prison, on drugs, or dead, but God has made him or her successful. Oh, the marvelous grace of God!

So Potiphar put Joseph in charge of everything in his house, and the Lord blessed Potiphar's house on account of Joseph. With Joseph in charge, Potiphar did not concern himself with anything in his house. We have seen in this book that God blesses others because of those who have found grace in His sight. We have seen that not only the consequences but the *blessings* of a family are transmitted to later generations. But the big point is that God blessed Joseph and all that he did—in spite of his family mess!

God can bless you in spite of your family mess, too. Family mess cannot thwart your destiny when you are trusting and obeying God.

Now the Bible gives us an editorial comment that sets up the action that is about to follow. It says that Joseph was handsome in form and in appearance. He had a nice looking body and face. Joseph was truly one of "The Bold and the Beautiful." And it got him in trouble.

"It came about after these events that his master's wife looked with desire at Joseph, and she said, 'Lie with me'" (Genesis 39:7). Potiphar's wife was lusting for sex with Joseph. She didn't say, "I think we can get together." She didn't say, "I like you; do you like me?" She said, "Lie with me." She was only looking for sex. That is kind of how things are today, isn't it? People are looking for sex, not love. She didn't love him; he was merely the object of her lust.

I've seen this phenomenon many times. Men who are blessed by God carry an anointing. They stand out. There is upon some men a special sense of Christ's presence or the Holy Spirit's working. And women are often attracted to that anointing. It is as if they are trying to capture the anointing, authority, or power of the anointing in that man. But they don't understand that if they capture it (outside of the will of God, that is) they will ruin it. Delilah tried to capture the anointing that drew her to Samson, but she ruined it instead. In the language of children's stories, it's like killing the goose that laid the golden eggs.

Joseph's response to Potiphar's wife is an example of great integrity:

> But he refused and said to his master's wife, "Behold, with me here, my master does not concern himself with anything in the house, and he has put all that he owns in my charge. There is

no one greater in this house than I, and he has withheld nothing from me except you, because you are his wife. How then could I do this great evil and sin against God?" As she spoke to Joseph day after day, he did not listen to her to lie beside her or be with her (Genesis 39:8–10).

He refused to lie with her because of the evil he would be perpetrating against his master's trust in him and His God. Joseph was concerned about the two things that will greatly reduce adultery: care for one's fellow man and care for God. If we were concerned about these two characteristics, adultery would virtually disappear.

Now I'm sure Potiphar's wife worked it well. She probably told him that no one had to know. She probably pointed out that there was no one around. She probably reminded him that he was not married and therefore wouldn't be cheating on his wife. But Joseph was a man of integrity, so he refused her.

Is that confusing to you? It is to me a little. When you look at Joseph's family background, I have to wonder where this integrity came from. He didn't get it from Abraham—he was a liar. He didn't get it from Isaac—he was passive. He certainly didn't get it from Jacob—he was a cheater from his mother's womb. So where did he get it from? It must have come from God's dream and Joseph's walk with God.

A lot of people want to tell me, "The reason I am where I am is because of my mother's nursing habits" or "The reason I am where I am is because somebody didn't do something for me when I was growing up." That is no excuse for not choosing a position of integrity. Joseph chose the path of integrity *in spite of* his family mess.

Have you ever been offered a tempting proposition? I have. How did you respond? How *are* you responding? You believe that you can't resist the temptation, but you will receive integrity from the dream, destiny, and walk with God!

Potiphar's wife didn't stop there. His rejection only made her want him more. She spoke to him day after day about this. Satan is persistent! He is going to proposition you day after day. I don't understand it when Christians act like something's wrong when Satan's attacking them. Get used to it: He's going to come back every day. The Bible says that when Jesus was driven by the Holy Spirit into the wilderness, Satan left Him—to return at an opportune time. Satan is always waiting and lurking. He's going to be after you day after day.

One day when Joseph went in to the house to do some work, he discovered that he was alone with Potiphar's wife. She had probably arranged it that way. So she grabbed his robe and said, "Lie with me!"

Joseph didn't try to think his way out of the situation. He didn't reason with her. He didn't pray about the situation. He didn't rebuke the devil. He ran and left his garment in her hand.

The first, best response to temptation is a good pair of tennis shoes and a burst of energy. We like to get all spiritual: "Oh, I'm praying about this. I'm praying about you!" Prayer isn't going to help you in some of those situations. You've got to run. Don't give the devil opportunity.

No doubt this infuriated Potiphar's wife. So she accused him of attempted rape. She broadcast her accusations to the men of her household. You can see that there was no love here, only lust. Love wants what is best for the other person, even at its own expense. Lust wants what it wants, when it wants it, even at the expense of the other person.

When Potiphar heard his wife's accusations, his anger burned. He believed that all his trust in Joseph had been repaid with treachery. So he threw Joseph into jail where the king's prisoners were confined.

What is going on?

What is going to happen to Joseph's dream?

Why would God allow something like this to happen?

It looked bad for Joseph, even though he had done the right thing. He was caught up in someone else's family mess. But by now you ought to know that if God has a destiny for you, it's going to come to pass. God needed Joseph in prison to work out His plan. As long as Joseph was Potiphar's servant, he could never be second in command of Egypt.

Sometimes God needs to put you in a personal prison, to work out His plan in your life. This is where most of us lose faith, become bitter, and let our confusion rob us of God's blessings. If God loves me, why is this painful thing happening?

But Joseph doesn't seem to have responded negatively. He simply continued to serve God in a new place. That's amazing to me.

In prison the same thing happened to Joseph that had happened to him in Potiphar's house: God began to prosper everything he did. So the chief jailer put everything in the whole jail under Joseph's supervision, and the Lord prospered everything that Joseph did.

God is able to work beneath, behind, through, above, and beyond family mess. He can bless you no matter where you are when you trust in Him, His dream, and His destiny for your life.

It was in prison that Joseph met Pharaoh's former cupbearer and former baker. These were positions of influence in Pharaoh's court. God sometimes sends us to strange places to make important contacts. One night the cupbearer and the baker both had a dream. When Joseph saw them in the morning, he noticed that they were dejected. So he asked them what the matter was.

The cupbearer told Joseph his dream. Then Joseph, by the power of God, interpreted that dream. He told the cupbearer that in three days Pharaoh would restore him to his post. He asked the cupbearer that when he was restored to the palace that he would remember Joseph there in the jail.

I believe that this was an attempt by Joseph to manipulate his situation to his advantage. He was using human means to try to effect God's plan. Of course it wouldn't work, but he tried anyway. Perhaps we're seeing a little of his father, Jacob the Cheater, seeping through.

Well, when the baker saw that the cupbearer's interpretation was favorable, he also told Joseph his dream. Joseph interpreted his dream, too, but the interpretation was unfavorable. He told him that in three days he would have his head cut off.

In three days, both dreams were fulfilled just as Joseph had interpreted them. It was Pharaoh's birthday. He had a feast for all his servants and he restored the cupbearer to the palace. But the baker was beheaded.

Now in those days the cupbearer was the royal taster of foods. His job was to be sure that no one would try to poison the king. He was sometimes an adviser and he was often in the presence of the king. But this man did not remember Joseph's request. Try as he might, Joseph could not manipulate the plan and timing of God, because God is sovereign.

Nor can you manipulate the plan and timing of God. You can't fix it. You can't turn it around. You can't make God do what you want Him to do. God is sovereign. He's got you where He wants you, because here is where He wants to work some things out. I hear people say, "I just think that I would be all right if I had another husband. I know He can work with this one, but..." But you can't fix that. That's God's hand. He'll work it out the way He wants to work it out. So you might as well leave it alone.

Well, after two more years, Pharaoh had a dream. It was only when nobody could interpret the dream that the cupbearer remembered Joseph and told Pharaoh about him. Pharaoh sent for Joseph, Joseph interpreted the dream, and Pharaoh elevated him to the second highest position in the land, second only to Himself. Please notice the progress of Joseph's life:

- Joseph—descendant of Jacob the trickster, Isaac the passive well-digger, and Abraham the reluctant father of faith—was now elevated by God to the second most powerful position in the world.

- Joseph—the favorite son of his father, the one who was hated by his brothers and sold into slavery—was elevated by God to the second most powerful position in the world.

- Joseph—who came from a family laden with family mess—was now elevated by God to the second most powerful position in the world. He became one of the greatest rulers of all time.

Little did Joseph's brothers know when they were plotting to kill him and sell him into slavery that they were sending him on his way to God's dream and destiny! Little do our family or church members know that when they plot to kill us with their mouths and when they sell us into slavery that they're sending us on our way to our destiny in Jesus Christ. God has a dream, a destiny, and a plan for your life. If you trust in God, even family mess can't stop it, because God works beneath, behind, through, in spite of, above, and beyond family mess. *God is greater than family mess!*

I want to look at two Scriptures that sum up God's work in spite of family mess in the life of Joseph:

> Now before the year of famine came, two sons were born to Joseph, whom Asenath, the daughter of Potiphera priest of On, bore to him. Joseph named the firstborn Manasseh, "For," he said, "God has made me forget all my trouble and all my father's household." He named the second Ephraim, "For," he said, "God has made me fruitful in the land of my affliction" (Genesis 41:50–52).

There are some good lessons for us here:

God can make you forget about all your trouble. He can make you forget about everything that happened in your past. That ought to excite you.

God can make you forget about your father's entire dysfunctional household. This doesn't mean that Joseph wouldn't have to deal with them anymore. Jehovah God sent all of his brothers to him, down in Egypt. It means that God can make you forget about them, as far as being the predominant, preoccupying, negative force in your life.

God can make you fruitful in the land of your affliction. People looked at Jesus and said, "Can anything good come out of Nazareth? Don't we know His mother? Isn't His mother's name Mary? Isn't His father named Joseph? I used to work with Joseph, down in the carpentry business. I know them. Nothing good can come out of there." But God said, "I'll take this boy and make something out of Him and lift Him up. I don't care what the world says about it, or how they look at Him." It works for you, too. God can take you and make something out of you. Praise God!

The second Scripture is a favorite of Bible readers. It is Joseph's response to his brothers after the death of his father. Since their father was dead, they wanted to know if Joseph was going to seek vengeance against them for everything they'd done to him.

> But Joseph said to them, "Do not be afraid, for am I in God's place? As for you, you meant evil against me, but God meant it for good in order to bring about this present result, to preserve many people alive" (Genesis 50:19–20).

Beloved, never usurp the place of God. *"Vengeance is mine,"* *says the Lord, "I will repay"* (Romans 12:19). God will take care of the hatred, cruelty, and mistreatment of your family. In addition, God will take the evil they work against you and work it to your good.

God is saying, "I'll take the evil that people do against you and turn it around and make it for your good." Have you ever experienced this? Somebody will go behind your back to smear you, but when they get done they're the ones who get smeared. Because God has taken what they said and turned it around and sent it another way to be able to work out what He wants to work out for you. There is no weapon formed against a Christian that can prosper when you are in God's will. *"God causes all things to work together for good to those who love God, to those who are called according to His purpose"* (Romans 8:28).

And finally, God will bring about His dream and destiny for your life through the family mess that He allows in your life. He will use family mess as a vehicle to put you in a place to preserve many people! God wants to use your family mess. He wants to use that thing that happened to you so that He can turn it around and make it a ministry.

Maybe you have been raped. That's a horrible, horrible thing! But God will take that rape and turn it around and give you a ministry out of rape, so that you can help people.

Maybe you've been abused—that's a horrible thing! God will take the abuse and turn it around and bless you and comfort you and give you a ministry working with people who have been abused.

God will take your divorce and, after you've been all messed up for five or six years, He will heal you and comfort you and turn you around and give you a ministry dealing with divorced people.

God will take you, all full of anger and clean you up out of that anger, turn you around, and give you a ministry comforting others with the comfort wherewith you yourself have been comforted. He'll take the evil that people do in your life and turn it around.

Hear it one last time: God works beneath, behind, through, above, and beyond family mess to bring you to your destiny. God is greater than family mess!

DISCUSSION QUESTIONS

1. How do you see God working beneath, behind, above, and beyond your family mess?

2. What is your spiritual dream?

3. How do you think God is going to fulfill your dream through your own personal family mess?

4. Share one of your difficult experiences that you believe will lead you towards your ultimate spiritual dream and destiny.

5. In what personal way do you see God being greater than your family mess?

CONCLUSION

Thanks for taking this Bible journey with me! We have traveled through valleys and over mountains. We have faced dangers and seen the providence of Almighty God. We have seen Abraham leave home under the direction of Jehovah God—not knowing where he was to go, but God guided him from the legacy of Babylonia. We explored the family mess between Sarah and Hagar, Isaac and Jacob, and Abraham and Sarah.

We have followed the trail of this family through the family mess of the twelve sons of Jacob. This was certainly a low point and a valley in the life of this family. But, we persisted and followed Joseph out of the valley of family mess onto the pinnacle of world leadership, through grace, providence, and blessings of Jehovah God.

We have learned on this journey that God is greater than family mess. God worked through, beneath, behind, above, beyond, and in spite of family mess to deliver Joseph to the mountaintop of his destiny. Neither Terah's idolatry, nor Abraham's passivity, nor Isaac's lying about his wife, nor Jacob's tricks, nor the treachery of Jacob's sons could keep God from lifting Joseph above this mess. Joseph was the one, through the grace and power of God, who broke the chain of family mess in his family.

You can be the one who breaks it in your family.

The soap operas never end, but this one ended in the way that life will end for all of us who trust God to walk with us through family mess: "And they lived happily ever after." Remember, God is greater than family mess!

THE FIRST STEP TO BREAKING THE CHAIN OF FAMILY MESS IS TRUSTING JESUS CHRIST AS YOUR SAVIOUR

If you want to take the first step to overcoming family mess in your life and begin living the victorious life God planned for you to live, here is how you can take that first step today:

1. **Accept the fact that you are a sinner, and that you have broken God's law.** The Bible says in Ecclesiastes 7:20: *"For there is not a just man upon earth that doeth good, and sinneth not."* Romans 3:23: *"For all have sinned and come short of the glory of God."*

2. **Accept the fact that there is a penalty for sin.** The Bible states in Romans 6:23: *"For the wages of sin is death…"*

3. **Accept the fact that you are on the road to hell.** Jesus Christ said in Matthew 10:28: *"And fear not them which kill the body, but are not able to kill the soul: but rather fear him which is able to destroy both soul and body in hell."*

The Bible says in Revelation 21:8: *"But the fearful, and unbelieving, and the abominable, and murderers, and whoremongers and sorcerers, and idolaters, and all liars, shall have their part in the lake which burneth with fire and brimstone: which is the second death."*

4. **Accept the fact that you cannot do anything to save yourself!** The Bible states in Ephesians 2: 8, 9: *"For by grace are ye saved through faith: and that not of yourselves: it is a gift of God. Not of works, lest any man should boast."*

5. **Accept the fact that God loves you more than you love yourself, and that He wants to save you from hell.** *"For God so loved the world, that He gave His only begotten Son, that whosoever believeth in Him should not perish, but have everlasting life"* (John 3:16).

6. With these facts in mind, please repent of your sins, believe on the Lord Jesus Christ and pray and ask Him to come into your heart and save you this very moment.

The Bible states in the book of Romans 10:9, 13: *"That if thou shalt confess with thy mouth the Lord Jesus, and shalt believe in thine heart that God hath raised Him from the dead, thou shalt be saved." "For whosoever shall call upon the name of the Lord shall be saved."*

7. If you are willing to trust Christ as your Saviour and receive the power of the Holy Ghost in your life, please pray with me the following prayer:

> Heavenly Father, I realize that I am a sinner and that I have sinned against you. For Jesus Christ's sake, please forgive me of all of my sins. I now believe with all of my heart that Jesus Christ died, was buried, and rose again for me. Lord Jesus, please come into my heart, save my soul, change my life, and fill me with your Holy Spirit today and forever. Amen.

NOTES

Disclaimer

1 Jerome H. Neyrey, Editor, The Social World Of Luke-Acts, (Hendrickson Publishers, Inc., Peabody, Massachusetts, 1991), p. xv.

2 Jerome H. Neyrey, Editor, The Social World Of Luke-Acts, Hendrickson Publishers, Inc., Peabody, Massachusetts, 1991, p. 9.

Chapter 1

1 Merriam-Webster Collegiate Dictionary (Zane Publishing, Inc., 1997).

2 Robert Hemfelt & Paul Warren, Kids Who Carry Our Pain (Thomas Nelson Publishers, Carmel, New York, 1990).

Chapter 2

1 Malcolm Smith, Spiritual Burnout (Pillar Books and Publishing Company, Tulsa, Oklahoma, 1995), 86.

Chapter 9

1 Pat Springle, Trusting (Servant Publications, Ann Arbor, Michigan, 1994), 132.

2 Gordan Wenham, Word Biblical Commentary, Volume 2, Genesis 16–50 (Word Books, Dallas, Texas, 1994), 295.

3 C. H. Mackintosh, Genesis to Deuteronomy, Notes on the Pentateuch

(Loizeaux Brothers, Neptune, New Jersey, 1972), 122.

4 Keil & Delitzsch, Commentary on the Old Testament, Volume I, The Pentateuch (William B. Eerdmans Publishing Company, Grand Rapids, Michigan, 1988), 306.

Chapter 11
1 John Friel and Linda Friel, Adult Children: The Secrets of Dysfunctional Families (Health Communications, Inc., Deerfield Beach, Florida, 1988), 155.

2 Ibid., 155–156.

3 Robert Hemfelt, Frank Minirith, Paul Meier, Love Is A Choice (Thomas Nelson Publishers, Nashville, Tennessee, 1989), 11.

4 Friel, 157.

5 Ibid., 74–75.

For More Information About
Bishop Joey Johnson's Ministry, Visit:

www.THOTL.org

Made in the USA
Middletown, DE
24 April 2015